P R E S E N T E D   T O :

_____

B Y :

_____

WISDOM

for the way

WISE WORDS FOR BUSY PEOPLE

CHARLES R.
SWINDOLL

WISDOM FOR THE WAY
Copyright © 2001 by Charles R. Swindoll

Published by J. Countryman, a division of Thomas Nelson, Inc,
Nashville, Tennessee 37214.

Compiled and edited by Terri Gibbs.

Unless otherwise indicated, all Scripture quotations in this book are from the
New American Standard Bible (NASB) © 1960, 1962, 1963, 1971, 1972, 1973,
1975, and 1977 by the Lockman Foundation, and are used by permission.

Other Scripture references are from the following sources:

The New International Version of the Bible (NIV) © 1984 by the International
Bible Society. Used by permission of Zondervan Bible Publishers.

The King James Version of the Bible (KJV).

The New King James Version (NKJV) ©1979, 1980, 1982, 1992,
Thomas Nelson, Inc., Publisher.

The Good News Bible: The Bible in Today's English Version (TEV)
© 1976 by the American Bible Society.

Designed by Uttley/Douponce DesignWorks, Sisters, Oregon.
Cover image: Bullaty-Lomeo/Image Bank

ISBN: 0-8499-9518-3

Printed and bound in Belgium

*It has been my distinct honor and joy
to serve as the president of
Dallas Theological Seminary since
the summer of 1994.*

*A major reason the seven-year journey
has been such a delight is due, in part,
to the pleasant relationship I have sustained
with the school's Board of Incorporate Members.*

*I dedicate this volume to that body
of faithful men and women who give wise
oversight to this outstanding institution.
The title and contents of this book
describe their kind of leadership. My life
is deeper because our paths have crossed.*

*May our Lord abundantly reward
them for their selfless devotion and
uncompromising integrity.*

*My love for each individual
knows no bounds.*

CONTENTS

We have not even begun to live if we lack the wisdom God wants to give to us. That wisdom is ours, simply for the asking, and it brings us into a whole new and exciting world! Like birth, it will take time and it may be a painful process. But when it comes, you'll be amazed how clearly things will come into focus. You'll begin to feel like a new creature. No wonder Jesus referred to it as being "born again."

When we operate in the sphere of the wisdom of God, when it is at work in our minds and in our lives, we look at life through lenses of perception, and we respond to it in calm confidence. There's a remarkable absence of fear. We are not seized with panic. We can either lose our jobs or we can be promoted in our work, and neither will derail us. Why? Because we see it with God-given objectivity. And we handle it in His wisdom.

We can dip into an unexpected valley or we can soar to the pinnacle of prosperity, and we can cope with both extremes. His wisdom provides us the necessary objectivity and stability. This is not some dreamland fantasy. It is reality. It is the ability to live above the drag of human opinion and horizontal perspective. It is what happens within us when wisdom goes to work.

The wisdom of God gives us *balance, strength,* and *insight.* None of these is a natural trait, each is a by-product of wisdom. We don't get these things just because we're human beings. They must come from God.

But the more we glean God's wisdom, the more strength we gain to live with questions and tension. He doesn't issue rules and regulations for every moment. He provides some overall guidelines and principles, then He allows us to make the decisions. Why? By doing this the wisdom of God goes to work, and we begin to learn how to walk through life—which is often full of subtle and unseen "land mines." His wisdom provides the sixth sense we need. It matures us so that we can press on in spite of the unanswered questions.

The good news is that such wisdom is ours to claim through an intimate relationship with God's Son, Jesus. He is the channel through which wisdom comes to us. In coming by faith to the Lord Jesus Christ, we are given open access to the wisdom of God. With the Son of God comes the wisdom of God. It's all part of the package.

Charles R. Swindoll

Wisdom

*Wisdom is the ability to
view life as God perceives it.*

No Success
Without Wisdom

Wisdom has the advantage of giving success.

ECCLESIASTES 10:10

I don't know of a hotter subject today than success. Magazine articles, books, seminars, and sermons promote it. But success is seldom linked with wisdom. Chances are good that if we would pick up last Sunday's paper and read it through, we'd come across twenty or more references to success, yet find nothing added regarding wisdom. In today's hype about success, wisdom is conspicuous by its absence. Outside of biblical literature and biblically based books, we hardly even come across the word. . . .

[Wisdom] may not give us great popularity and wealth and it may not mean that we will be the most respected in our field or that we will have the most significant voice in the company, but ultimately, as God gauges it, we will be successful.

Living on the Ragged Edge

The ABCs of Love

Hatred stirs up strife,
but love covers all transgression.

PROVERBS 10:12

"I **a**ccept you as you are."
"I **b**elieve you are valuable."
"I **c**are when you hurt."
"I **d**esire only what is best for you."
"I **e**rase all offenses."

We could call that the ABC's of love. And I don't know of anybody who would turn his back on such magnetic, encouraging statements.

There is nothing shallow about authentic love. Nor is it a magic wand we whip out and wave over a problem with a whoosh, hoping all the pain will go away. Real love has staying power. Authentic love is tough love. It refuses to look for ways to run away. It always opts for working through. It doesn't cop out because the sea gets stormy and rough. It's fibrous and resilient. . . . While the world around us gives the opposite counsel, love stands firm.

Dropping Your Guard

Real Riches

In [Christ] are hidden all the
treasures of wisdom and knowledge.

Colossians 2:3

From the looks of things, you're pretty impressive. You've got a nice place. And I suppose your neighbors would agree that you're a hard worker . . . climbing right on up that ladder toward success, right? . . .

Your salary is good and your material possessions are growing in number, but . . . the truth is you are empty on the inside and you're faking it on the outside. Not one thing you own in your "kingdom" has brought you the happiness you long for. So you're thinking, "Maybe if I could land that better job," or "get into that bigger house," or . . . or . . . .

But don't allow the smoke screen of more money to blind your eyes to the truth. There's a lot more to being rich than making more money. Seneca, the Roman, was right "Money has never yet made anyone rich." Do you want riches? Then listen to Jesus: *But seek first His kingdom and His righteousness; and all these things shall be added to you* (Matt. 6:33).

For the *real* riches, try switching kingdoms.

Living on the Ragged Edge

Power to Overcome

Apply your heart to discipline
and your ears to words of knowledge.

PROVERBS 23:12

Can't and *won't*. Christians need to be very careful which one they choose. It seems that we prefer to use "can't."

"I just can't get along with my wife."

"My husband and I can't communicate."

"I just can't discipline the kids as I should."

"I just can't give up the affair I'm having."

"I can't stop overeating."

"I can't find time to pray."

Any Christian who takes the Bible seriously will have to agree the word here really should be "won't." Why? Because we have been given the power, the ability to overcome. . . .

We're really saying "I won't," because we don't choose to say "With the help of God, I will!"

Day by Day with Charles Swindoll

God's Plan for Hope

For I know the plans I have for you . . .
plans to prosper you and not harm you,
plans to give you hope and a future.

JEREMIAH 29:11, NIV

God knows, right down to the final nub, exactly where you are in life. He sees. He cares. He is aware. And best of all, He is touched by it.

The enemy of our souls wants you to think differently. *God doesn't care. He's left you in this mess for so many months. How unfair! Those around you, those at work, your neighbors, live like the devil, and they're making it fine. And here you don't even have a job. You don't even have enough to cover the credit card bills. What kind of God is that?*

Or maybe some young mother-to-be, stretched to the limit already with other young children and crushing responsibilities, cries out in her heart, "My situation is more than I can bear!" And God replies, "My daughter, I know what I am doing. I know the pain of your heart right now. I know you feel overwhelmed, overloaded, pressed down. But believe Me, I am touched with your situation. And I have a plan! I am working out the details of your deliverance even now. Trust Me!"

Moses: A Man of Selfless Dedication

Five Cheers for Mom

*She looks well to the ways of
her household; . . . her children rise up
and bless her, her husband also.*

PROVERBS 31:27–28.

What does motherhood require? Transparent tenderness, authentic spirituality, inner confidence, unselfish love, and self-control. Quite a list, isn't it? Almost more than we should expect. Perhaps that explains why Erma Bombeck used to say that motherhood takes 180 movable parts and 3 pairs of hands and 3 sets of eyes . . . and, I might add, the grace of God. If you happen to be a mother, here's one guy who applauds your every effort. Five cheers for all you do! . . .

Remember the Skin Horse in *The Velveteen Rabbit?* All his stuffing was starting to come out, his hair had been "loved off," but how valuable he was! . . . Carefully kept mothers don't have secure kids. Carefully kept, untouchable "velveteen mothers" turn out fragile, selfish, untouchable children. But unselfish, giving, secure moms somehow manage to deposit healthy, wholesome kids into our lonely, frightened society.

Growing Wise in Family Life

God's New Morning Message

The LORD raises up those
who are bowed down;
the LORD loves the righteous.

PSALM 146:8

Do you know what God's fresh, new morning message is to us? Whether the sun is shining brightly or whether it's pouring down rain? Whether the morning is bright or whether it's gray and overcast? His promise is the dawn itself. . . . Every morning the Lord comes through with His encouraging message, "We're still on speaking terms, you know! I'm here. I haven't moved. Let's go together today." . . .

Trust God to remember you. He won't forget your name. He won't forget your circumstances, He certainly won't forget your prayers. . . . Trust Him, He remembers you.

The Mystery of God's Will

No Fear of Failure

The wicked flee when no one is pursuing,
but the righteous are bold as a lion.

PROVERBS 28:1

When will we ever learn that there are no hopeless situations, only people who have grown hopeless about them? What appears as an unsolvable problem to us is actually a rather exhilarating challenge. People who inspire others are those who see invisible bridges at the end of dead-end streets.

There was a Cabinet meeting in London during the darkest days of the Second World War. France had just capitulated. Prime Minister Churchill outlined the situation in its starkest colors. Quite literally, the tiny British Isles stood alone. Grim faces stared back at him in stoic silence. Despair and thoughts of surrender were written in their looks. The visionary statesman momentarily remained silent, lit a cigar, showed a hint of a smile, and with a twinkle in his eye, responded to that dispirited company of officials, "Gentlemen, I find it rather inspiring." . . . What a great line! No wonder people followed the man. Fear of failure never entered his mind!

Dropping Your Guard

A Loving Father

How blessed are the people who know
the joyful sound! . . . O LORD, they walk
in the light of Your countenance.

PSALM 89:15

Contrary to popular opinion, God doesn't sit in heaven with His jaws clenched, His arms folded in disapproval, and a deep frown on His brow. He is not ticked off at His children for all the times we trip over our tiny feet and fall flat on our diapers. He is a loving Father, and we are precious in His sight, the delight of His heart. After all, He "has qualified us to share in the inheritance of the saints in light" (Col. 1:12). Think of it! He's put us in His inheritance!

Remember that the next time you think God is coming down on you. You have reason to give thanks. You don't have to qualify yourself for His kingdom. His grace has rescued you.

Hope Again

Precepts and Principles

Teach me good discernment and knowledge,
for I believe in Thy commandments.

PSALM 119:66

❧ Whenever you see the scriptural phrase "This is the will of God," you know for sure that's God's will. You also know that to disobey is to break His Word. Other clear indications of His leading are the precepts and principles in the Scripture.

Precepts are clearly marked statements like "Abstain from sexual immorality." That's like saying, "Speed Limit 35." What is speeding? Anything over thirty-five miles an hour. That's a precept.

Then there are *principles* . . . and these are general guidelines that require discernment and maturity if we are to grasp them. . . . Like the sign that says, "Drive carefully." This may mean forty miles an hour on a clear, uncongested highway, or it may mean ten miles an hour on an ice-covered curve. But it always means that we must be alert and aware of conditions; it always means we have to be discerning. . . . These principles require wisdom and discernment.

The Mystery of God's Will

Friendly People, Thoughtful People

There is a friend who
sticks closer than a brother.

PROVERBS 18:24

If I have learned anything during my journey on Planet Earth, it is that people need one another. The presence of other people is essential—caring people, helpful people, interesting people, friendly people, thoughtful people. These folks take the grind out of life. About the time we are tempted to think we can handle things all alone—boom! We run into some obstacle and need assistance. We discover all over again that we are not nearly as self-sufficient as we thought.

In spite of our high-tech world and efficient procedures, people remain the essential ingredient of life. When we forget that, a strange thing happens: We start treating people like inconveniences instead of assets.

Laugh Again

Don't Get Burned!

Bad company corrupts good morals.

1 CORINTHIANS 15:33

Compromise never works. We always get burned. Even though we rationalize around our weak decisions and tell ourselves that wicked associations really won't harm us ("they'll get better, our good will rub off their *bad!*"), we get soiled in the process.

If you put on a pair of clean white gloves on a rainy day and then go out into the backyard to the flowerbed and pick up a glob of mud, trust me, the mud will never get "glovey." The gloves will definitely get muddy. Every time. In all my sixty-plus years on earth, I have never seen glovey mud. Not once. In simple terms, that's what 1 Corinthians 15:33 is saying: "Do not be deceived: 'Bad company corrupts good morals.'"

Dropping Your Guard

Pull in the Anchor

Forgive us our debts, as we
also have forgiven our debtors.

MATTHEW 6:12

Have you done someone wrong? Have you been offensive? Have your actions caused hurt? To do nothing is not only in direct disobedience to Jesus' teaching, it also complicates your life. It adds heavier mental weights than you are capable of carrying. It is like dropping an anchor and then cranking up your boat's engine and putting it in gear. The anchor keeps catching and snagging on the bottom, making for a terribly uncomfortable ride across the water. How simple the solution! Just pull in the anchor. . . .

Let me give you a simple tip: We cannot be right with God until we are right with others.

Simple Faith

Segments of Solitude

My soul, wait in silence for
God only, for my hope is from Him.

Henri Nouwen called solitude . . . "the furnace of transformation." This doesn't refer to mere personal privacy for a twelve-second pit stop where we get a quick fix to reenter the race. It's more than that. It's an oasis of the soul where we see ourselves, others, and especially our God in new ways. It's where much of the "clutter" of life is identified and exterminated, thanks to the merciless heat of the "furnace." Soul surgery transpires as serenity replaces anxiety.

In solitude, struggles occur that no one else knows about. Inner battles are fought here that seldom become fodder for sermons or illustrations for books. God, who probes our deepest thoughts during protracted segments of solitude, opens our eyes to things that need attention. It is here He makes us aware of those things we try to hide from others.

Intimacy with the Almighty

WISDOM FOR THE WAY   31

God's Hand on Your Life

My frame was not hidden from You,
when I was made in secret, and skillfully
wrought in the depths of the earth.

❧ Perhaps you never knew what it was to nestle securely in a parent's love. Your home life may have been strained or even fractured from your earliest memory. From a human point of view, your birth might have come at a difficult or awkward time in your parents' lives. It may be that you've never known the reassurance of a faithful mother and father who built their faith into your heart. When you think back on your growing up years, you realize you don't have much to shout about.

I'd like to deliver a beautiful message to you, my friend. God's hand on your life may be just beginning to make its mark. That steep hill you've been climbing for such a long time may be the ramp to a destiny beyond your dreams. I do not believe there is any such thing as an accidental or ill-timed birth. You may have arrived in a home that was financially strapped. You may have known brokenness, hurt, and insecurity since your earliest days— but please hear me on this: *You were not an accident.*

Moses: A Man of Selfless Dedication

Giving God First Place

The LORD possessed me
at the beginning of His way,
before His works of old.

If some corporate position is the god of your life, then something terrible occurs within when it is no longer a future possibility. If your career, however, is simply a part of God's plan and you keep it in proper perspective, you can handle a demotion just as well as you can handle a promotion. It all depends on who's first and what's first.

Breaking the magnet that draws things ahead of God is a lengthy and sometimes painful process. There is a line found in the Jewish Talmud that puts it well: "Man is born with his hands clenched; he dies with them wide open. Entering life, he desires to grasp everything; leaving the world, all he possessed has slipped away." . . .

Just remember: Whatever is in first place, if it isn't Christ alone, it is in the wrong place.

Living Above the Level of Mediocrity

Alone with God

Thus the Lord GOD, . . . has said,
". . . In quietness and trust is your strength."

ISAIAH 30:15

✿ Some of the most profound ministries of the Spirit of God are not public or loud or large. Sometimes His most meaningful touch on our lives comes when we are all alone.

I urge you to include in your schedule time to be alone with God. . . . You do have places where you can get away for a long walk, don't you? I hope it's in a wooded area. The gentle breeze blowing through the forest is therapeutic. Sometimes just being alone out in God's marvelous creation is all that's needed for the scales to be removed from your eyes and for you to silence the harassment and the noise of your day and begin to hear from God.

Flying Closer to the Flame

It Is Finished

> *For all have sinned and fall short of*
> *the glory of God, being justified as a gift*
> *by His grace through the redemption*
> *which is in Christ Jesus.*
>
> ROMANS 3:23–24

Stop and think: Upon believing in Jesus Christ's substitutionary death and bodily resurrection, the once-lost sinner is instantly, unconditionally, and permanently "declared 100% righteous." Anything less and we are not righteous . . . we're *almost* righteous.

If we are declared 99.9% righteous, some verses of the Bible would have to be rewritten. Like Isaiah 1:18, which might then read: "'Come now, and let us reason together,' says the Lord, 'though your sins are as scarlet, they will be light pink.'"

Nonsense! The promise of sins forgiven is all or nothing. Eighty percent won't cut it. . . .

When our Lord said "It is finished," He meant "finished."

The Finishing Touch

Two Are Better Than One

Two are better than one because
they have a good return for their labor.

ECCLESIASTES 4:9

Independence is our watchword and "Think for Yourself" is our motto. Declaring a need is a sign of weakness, an open admission of failure and lack of character. Furthermore, we are on the move so much, who has time to share and to care? It has been my observation that we Christians are not immune from this hurry-up, hassle-hustle mentality. . . .

Even though it is easy to buy into the selfish lifestyle and opt for isolationism instead of involvement, the consequences are bitter and inescapable. . . . Swimming with the current of today's me-ism mindset has a way of eclipsing the contrasting light of Scripture.

"Two are better than one . . ." because:

- they have a good return for their labor—*mutual effort*
- one will lift up his companion—*mutual support*
- they keep (each other) warm—*mutual encouragement*
- they can resist an attack—*mutual strength*

Dropping Your Guard

Honest to the Core

Keep my commandments and live,
and my teaching as the apple of your eye.

PROVERBS 7:2

What is God looking for? He is looking for men and women whose hearts are completely His—*completely*. . . .

God is not looking for magnificent specimens of humanity. He's looking for deeply spiritual, genuinely humble, honest-to-the-core servants who have integrity. . . .

Today, we live in a world that says, in many ways, "If you just make a good impression, that's all that matters." But you will never be a man or woman of God if that's your philosophy. Never. You cannot fake it with the Almighty. He is not impressed with externals. He always focuses on the inward qualities . . . those things that take time and discipline to cultivate.

David: A Man of Passion and Destiny

A Well-Chosen Word

A word fitly spoken, is like
apples of gold in pictures of silver.

PROVERBS 25:11, KJV

Like Jell-O, concepts assume the mold of the words into which they are poured. Who has not been stabbed awake by the use of a particular word . . . or combinations of words? Who has not found relief from a well-timed word spoken at the precise moment of need? Who has not been crushed beneath the weight of an ill-chosen word? And who has not gathered fresh courage because a word of hope penetrated the fog of self-doubt? The term *word* remains the most powerful of all four-letter words.

Colors fade.

Shorelines erode.

Temples crumble. Empires fall. But "a word fitly spoken" endures.

Simple Faith

The Secret Is Acceptance

I will put my trust in Him.

HEBREWS 2:13

Helen Rosevcare was a British medical missionary in the Congo years ago during an uprising. Her faith was strong and her trust was confident, yet she was raped and assaulted and treated brutally. Commenting later, she said, "I must ask myself a question as if it came directly from the Lord. 'Can you thank Me for trusting you with this experience even if I never tell you why?'"

What a profound thought. God has trusted each of us with our own set of unfair circumstances and unexplained experiences to deal with. Can we still trust in Him even if He never tells us why?

The secret to responsible trust is *acceptance*. Acceptance is taking from God's hand absolutely anything He gives, looking into His face in trust and thanksgiving, knowing that the confinement of the hedge we're in is good and for His glory.

Perfect Trust

Dangerous Disillusionment

The steadfast of mind
You will keep in perfect peace,
because he trusts in You.

ISAIAH 26:3

Disillusionment is a dangerous, slippery slope. First we become disillusioned about our fellow man. Then we move on to cynicism. Before long, we trust no one, not even God. We've been burned. We've been taken advantage of; we've been mistreated. . . .

The cause of disillusionment and the cure for it can be expressed in almost the sample simple words. The cause of disillusionment is *putting one's complete hope and trust in people.* Putting people on a pedestal, focusing on them, finding our security in them. . . .And when the feet of clay crumble (as they surely will) total disillusionment sets in.

What's the cure? *Putting our complete hope and trust in the living Lord.* When we do that, the simplest messages from God calm our spirits.

Joseph: A Man of Integrity and Forgiveness

Heavenly Hindsight

You are my hiding place;
You preserve me from trouble;
You surround me with songs of deliverance.

PSALM 32:7

🌿 *Providence.* We toss the word around. But have you ever analyzed it? It comes from the Latin, *providentia.* Pro means "before" or "ahead of time"; *videntia* is from *videre*, meaning "to see." . . . Put them together and you have "seeing ahead of time," which is what Almighty God does. He sees the events of life ahead of time—something that we of course can never do.

We're great at history. Our hindsight is almost always 20/20. But we're lousy at prophecy, that is, the specifics of the future. Stop and think. We've no clue as to what will happen one minute from now, no idea what's going to happen next. But our invisible God, in His *providentia*, is continually, constantly, and confidently at work. . . .

He never changes. He knows what He is about, and He pursues it with relentless determination.

Esther: A Woman of Strength and Dignity

Checking Up on Your Job

*The soul of the sluggard craves
and gets nothing. But the soul
of the diligent is made fat.*

A young fellow rushed into a gas station to use the pay phone. The manager overheard his telephone conversation as he asked: "Sir, could you use a hardworking, honest young man to work for you?" [pause] "Oh . . . you've already got a hardworking, honest young man? Well, thanks anyway!"

The boy hung up the phone with a smile. Humming to himself, he began to walk away, obviously happy.

"How can you be so cheery?" asked the eavesdropping manager. "I thought the man you talked to already had someone and didn't want to hire you."

The young fellow answered, "Well, you see I *am* the hardworking young man. I was just checking up on my job!"

If you called your Boss, disguised your voice, and asked about your job, what do you think would be His answer?

Living Beyond the Daily Grind

Moral Character

A good name is to be
more desired than great wealth,
favor is better than silver and gold.

PROVERBS 22:1

Unfortunately, we have grown accustomed to shrugging off lapses in moral character, manifested in secretive and deceptive lifestyles. We are frequently told that trying to find people who value honesty and model responsibility, who promote fairness, accountability, loyalty, respect for others, and who hold to strong, upright convictions is not at all realistic.

"Such people don't exist . . . we need to stop requiring personal purity," we are told. Or, as one air-headed soul said during one recent presidential campaign, "We're voting for president, not pope."

To such an analogy, I reply "Nonsense!" That kind of logic (or rather, lack of logic) gives me the jitters.

Day by Day with Charles Swindoll

Celebrate Life!

Teach us to number our days aright,
that we may gain a heart of wisdom.

Psalm 90:12, niv

The Hebrew text suggests that we correctly "account" for our days. I find it interesting that we are to view life by the days, not *the years*. We are to live those days in such a way that when they draw to a close, we have gained "a heart of wisdom." With the Lord God occupying first place in our lives we accept and live each day enthusiastically for Him. The result will be that "heart of wisdom" the psalmist mentions. . . .

Because we cannot alter the inevitable, we adjust to it. And we do that not a year at a time, but a day at a time. Instead of eating our heart out because a few more aches and pains have attached themselves to our bodies, we determine to celebrate life rather than endure it. Aging isn't a choice. But our response to it is. In so many ways we ourselves determine how we shall grow old.

Strengthening Your Grip

God's Instruction Book

We know that the Son of God has come,
and has given us understanding so that
we may know Him who is true.

1 JOHN 5:20

God offers instruction, but then it's our move. We must accept His instruction and apply it to our lives. Then, and only then, can we expect to cash in on the benefits of His instruction. So you see, application is the essential link between instruction and change. . . .

God has sent us His instruction. He has preserved every word of it in a book, the Bible. It's all there, just as He communicated it to us. When He returns for His own, He isn't going to ask us how much we memorized or how often we met for study. No, He will want to know, "What did you do about my instructions?"

Living Above the Level of Mediocrity

Give God Your Worries

*Who is among you that
fears the LORD, . . . let him trust in the
name of the LORD and rely on his God.*

ISAIAH 50:10

Let's get six words clearly fixed in our minds.
These six words form the foundation of God's
therapeutic process for all worrywarts.

WORRY ABOUT NOTHING,

PRAY ABOUT EVERYTHING

What qualifies as a worry? Anything that
drains your tank of joy—something you cannot
change, something you are not responsible for,
something you are unable to control, something
(or someone) that frightens and torments you,
agitates you, keeps you awake when you should be
asleep. All of that now needs to be switched from
your worry list to your prayer list. Give each
worry—one by one—to God. . . . Tell Him you will
no longer keep your anxiety to yourself. . . .

The more you practice giving your mental
burdens to the Lord, the more exciting it gets to see
how God will handle the things that are impossible
for you to do anything about.

Laugh Again

The Sweet Taste of Success?

He who trusts in his riches
will fall, but the righteous will
flourish like the green leaf.

PROVERBS 11:28

Our society has gorged itself on the sweet taste of success. We've filled our plates from a buffet of books that range from dressing for success to investing for success. . . . We've gobbled down stacks of notebooks, cassette albums, and video tapes in our hunger for greater success.

The irony of all this is that . . . instead of fulfillment, we experience the bloated sensation of being full of ourselves—*our* dreams, *our* goals, *our* plans, *our* projects, *our* accomplishments. The result of this all-you-can-eat appetite is not contentment. It's nausea.

Hope Again

Free of Stress

Trust in Him always, O people;
pour your heart out before Him;
God is a refuge for us.

PSALM 62:8

You and I could name things, specific things that we've gone through in the last several years that make no logical sense whatsoever . . . but that's okay. We can't figure them out. But let me assure you, God is at work doing His mysterious plan (mysterious to us), which defies human logic. So quit trying to make it humanly logical. Trust Him. . . .

Do you realize what a peaceful life you can live if you decide to live like this? Do you realize how relaxed you can be, how free of stress? Honestly. It's so helpful for me to remind myself: He is the One who is unfathomable. He is unsearchable. I'm neither.

The Mystery of God's Will

Wisdom

A wise person goes God's way.
A fool doesn't.

No Island of Second Chance

Grandchildren are the crown of old men,
and the glory of sons is their fathers.

PROVERBS 17:6

We cannot change the past . . . and that includes the way we reared our children. All of us— yes, every parent I have ever met—would love to step into the time tunnel and return to the Island of Second Chance. We would give anything to relive those years and correct the failures and mistakes we committed the first time around. All such fantasy wishes need to be erased. They can never be fulfilled! The parenting process offers only one try per child, one day at a time, never again to be repeated.

Someone once said, "Life is like a coin; you can spend it any way you wish, but you spend it only once." That is never more true than with rearing children. About the time we get fairly good at it, our kids are all young adults and gone. Having come closer than ever to perfecting the process, we suddenly realize nobody is listening! Which means we're qualified for one major role: grandparenting (when it becomes our right to break all the rules and spoil those darlings!). It's a funny world.

Growing Wise in Family Life

A Fruitful Life

We have not ceased to pray for you; . . .
that you will walk in a manner worthy
of the Lord, to please Him in all respects,
bearing fruit in every good work. . . .

COLOSSIANS 1:9–10

Have you ever been in an area of the country where there was a lot of fruit ripening in the sun? Maybe on some cool September morning you've taken a walk through the apple orchards of the Hood River valley, or along the Columbia River in Oregon. It is pleasing to the eye to see such an abundance of sweet, delicious fruit hanging on branch or vine, ready to be plucked.

A fruitful Christian life is like that—sweet, refreshing, nourishing, fragrant, sustaining, delightful to be near. But such a life requires careful cultivation. . . . A deeper, more consistent walk with Christ requires time and attention every day. If that happens, you will bear fruit.

Moses: A Man of Selfless Dedication

Full of Grace and Truth

Grace and truth were
realized through Jesus Christ.

JOHN 1:17

While thinking back on his days with Jesus, John (one of The Twelve) remembers there was something about Him that was like no one else, during which time His disciples "beheld His glory." His uniqueness was that incredible "glory," a glory that represented the very presence of God. In addition, this glorious One was "full of grace and truth." Pause and let that sink in. It was His glory mixed with grace and truth that made Him different. In a world of darkness and demands, rules and regulations, requirements and expectations demanded by hypocritical religious leaders, Jesus came and ministered in a new and different way— He alone, full of grace and full of truth, introduced a revolutionary, different way of life.

Remembering that uniqueness, John adds, "For of His fullness we have all received, and grace upon grace" (John 1:16).

The Grace Awakening

"Good Job!"

How precious also are Your
thoughts to me, O God!
How vast is the sum of them.

PSALM 139:17

Most of us are good at criticizing ourselves and finding fault with what we have done or failed to do. I'd like to suggest an alternate plan—spend some of your leisure time finding pleasure and satisfaction in what you have done as well as in who and what you are. Sound too liberal? Why? Since when is a good self-esteem liberal?

There are times we need to tell ourselves, "Good job!" when we know that is true. That isn't conceited pride, my friend. It's acknowledging in words the feelings of the heart. The Lord knows that we hear more than enough internal put-downs! Communicating in times of leisure includes self-affirmation, acknowledging, of course, that God ultimately gets the glory. After all, He's the One who makes the whole experience possible.

Strengthening Your Grip

Savor Satisfaction

The beginning of wisdom is:
Acquire wisdom; and with all your
acquiring, get understanding.

The good life—the one that truly satisfies—exists only when we stop wanting a better one. It is the condition of savoring what *is* rather than longing for what might be. The itch for things, the lust for more—so brilliantly injected by those who peddle them—is a virus draining our souls of happy contentment. Have you noticed? A man never earns enough. A woman is never beautiful enough. Clothes are never fashionable enough. Cars are never nice enough. Gadgets are never modern enough. Houses are never furnished enough. Food is never fancy enough. Relationships are never romantic enough. Life is never full enough.

Satisfaction comes when we step off the escalator of desire and say, "This is enough. What I have will do. What I make of it is up to me and my vital union with the living Lord."

Moses: A Man of Selfless Dedication

Money Can't Buy Everything

How much better it is to get wisdom
than gold! And to get understanding
is to be chosen above silver.

PROVERBS 16:16

Foolish indeed is the person who considers himself safe and sound because he has money. . . .

And another reason it's foolish to trust in riches for security is that money, in the final analysis, brings no lasting satisfaction, certainly not in the area of things that really matter. There are many things that no amount of money can buy. Think of it this way:

- Money can buy medicine, but not health.
- Money can buy a house, but not a home.
- Money can buy companionship, but not friends.
- Money can buy food, but not an appetite.
- Money can buy a bed, but not sleep.
- Money can buy the good life, but not eternal life.

It is God (alone) who is able to supply us "with all things to enjoy." As Seneca, the Roman statesman once said: "Money has never yet made anyone rich."

Strengthening Your Grip

God—Incomprehensible!

Holy, Holy, Holy, is the LORD of Hosts,
the whole earth is full of His glory.

ISAIAH 6:3

What are the benefits of realizing God Incomprehensible? We no longer reduce Him to manageable terms. We are no longer tempted to manipulate Him and His will . . . or defend Him and His ways. Like the grieving prophet, we get new glimpses of Him "lofty and exalted," surrounded by legions of seraphim who witness Him as "Lord of Hosts" as they shout forth His praises in antiphonal voice (Isa. 6:1–2).

In a world consumed with thoughts of itself, filled with people impressed with each other, having disconnected with the only One worthy of praise, it's time we return to Theology 101 and sit silently in His presence. It's time we catch a fresh glimpse of Him who, alone, is awesome—incomprehensible.

Day by Day with Charles Swindoll

Sunrise, Sunset

The advantage of knowledge is that wisdom preserves the lives of its possessors.

ECCLESIASTES 7:12

God has given mankind the ability to see beyond the present. And He has not given that ability to any other creation. He has given us eternity in our hearts, without which "man will not find out the work which God has done from the beginning even to the *end*."

I have italicized "the end" for the sake of emphasis. Let me tell you why. It doesn't take a lot of brains to realize that if there is a sunrise, there must also be a sunset. To borrow from the astronaut's word, if there is an "earthrise," there must also be an "earthset."

So let's take that one step further. If there is an earth beginning, there must also be an earth ending. And if I'm existing on this boring earth without God, then I'm certainly not ready for an earth ending when I must face the One who made me.

Living on the Ragged Edge

The Weight of Worry

Casting all your anxiety on Him,
because He cares for you.

1 PETER 5:7

How wonderful that God personally cares about those things that worry us and prey upon our thoughts. He cares about them more than we care about them. Not a single nagging, aching, worrisome, stomach-tensing, blood-pressure-raising thought escapes His notice.

This is how the Phillips translation renders 1 Peter 5:7: "You can throw the whole weight of your anxieties upon him, for you are his personal concern."

Isn't that good? He genuinely cares. He is able to bear all the weight of your worry. Because you are His personal concern, you never disappear from His radar screen.

Moses: A Man of Selfless Dedication

Reach Out to Others

The generous man will be prosperous,
and he who waters will himself be watered.

PROVERBS 11:25

Close, open relationships are vital. A glib "Hi,
how are ya" must be replaced with genuine concern. The key term is *assimilation*. When I use the
word here, I'm referring to people reaching out to
one another.

Being absorbed in the function of the family of
God as a participant (rather than a spectator)
. . . relating to
. . . working with
. . . caring for others whom I know and love.
As I read it over, I see written between the lines
the reminder:
This is
   not
      automatic.
I am personally responsible.
So are you!

Dropping Your Guard

Wonderfully Made

I will give thanks to You, for I am fearfully and wonderfully made; wonderful are Your works, and my soul knows it very well.

🌿 The next time you pick up your little baby or grandbaby, look into the face of that marvelously made child and say, "You are fearfully and wonderfully made." And it wouldn't hurt to repeat that statement throughout her childhood. Children need to know how valuable they are in God's sight—and ours. Nothing gives them greater security than a strong sense of self-esteem.

Hear this well, busy parents—especially you who tend toward impatience, who are always on the run. . . . Your children have been put together in an altogether unique fashion, like no one else on earth. . . . They need you to help convince them they are unique persons, each one different, each one his or her own person. Children arrive in our arms longing to be known, longing to accept themselves as they are, to be who they are. So when they wade into the swift current of their times, they will be able to stand firm, and won't depend on peer pressure to give them their standard.

Growing Wise in Family Life

The Object of God's Concern

My soul waits in silence for God only;
from Him is my salvation.

PSALM 62:1

🌿 I've had times when I've found myself wondering about the things I've believed and preached for years. What happened? Had God died? No. My vision just got a little blurry. My circumstances caused my thinking to get a little foggy. I looked up, and I couldn't see Him as clearly.

That's what happened to John Bunyan back in the seventeenth century in England. He preached against the godlessness of his day, and the authorities shoved him into prison. . . . But because Bunyan firmly believed God was still alive and working, he turned that prison into a place of praise, service, and creativity as he began to write *Pilgrim's Progress,* the most famous allegory in the history of the English language.

When we hit a tough spot, our tendency is to feel abandoned. . . . In fact, just the opposite is true, for at that moment, we are more than ever the object of God's concern.

Elijah: A Man of Heroism & Humility

Take Life as It Comes

Sow your seed in the morning,
and do not be idle in the evening,
for you do not know whether morning
or evening sowing will succeed.

The only way we can come to terms with reality—is by trusting God, *regardless.* No ifs, ands, or buts. If I am a farmer and God allows a flood to come and wash away my crops or God chooses to give me the beautiful season rains and a bumper crop, I trust Him and I give Him praise. If I am in industry or some profession and someone throws me a curve and God allows my whole world to be reversed, I trust Him and I give Him praise. I take life as it occurs. I don't waste time in the pit of doubt. Nor do I worry over crop failures and strikeouts.

We can't wait for conditions to be perfect. Nor can we wait for things to be free of all risks—absolutely free, absolutely safe. Instead of protecting ourselves, we have to release ourselves. Instead of hoarding, we are to give and invest. Instead of drifting, we are to pursue life. Instead of doubting, we are to courageously trust.

Living on the Ragged Edge

God's Way Is Right

Trust in the LORD forever,
for in GOD the LORD,
we have an everlasting Rock.

God's way is always right. It doesn't always make sense—in fact . . . it is often mysterious. It can seldom be explained. It isn't always pleasurable and fun. But I have lived long enough to realize that His way is always right. . . .

I believe that not until we embrace God's sovereignty will we have the ability to reason our way through life. Until then we will be *too* important in the plan. Man's opinion will be *too* significant to us. And we will churn and wrestle and struggle our way through this Christian life, trying too hard to please people rather than living it relieved and relaxed in His plan.

The Mystery of God's Will

God Knows Our Limits

But You, O LORD, are a God
merciful and gracious, slow to anger and
abundant in lovingkindness and truth.

PSALM 86:15

Our Lord understands our limits. He realizes our struggles. He knows how much pressure we can take. He knows what measures of grace and mercy and strength we'll require. He knows how we're put together.

Frankly, His expectations are not nearly as unrealistic as ours. When we don't live up to the agenda we have set, we feel like He is going to dump a truckload of judgment on us. But that will not happen. So why do we fear it could?

Hope Again

Unity and Humility

> *Behold, how good and pleasant it*
> *is for brothers to dwell together in unity!*
>
> PSALM 133:1

Do you realize how closely unity and humility are tied together. One breeds the other; neither can exist without the other. They're like Siamese twins, perpetually connected. Personally, I have seen numerous occasions when pride won out (even though it was never called that) and harmony faded away . . . and I mean fast. . . .

Contrary to the stuff you might read today, the words, *fight* and *quarrel*, are not apt descriptions of the way to get ahead. They won't ultimately glorify God. Friends are made *not* fighting and by *refusing* to quarrel.

Commit yourself to freeing others so they can grow and discover on their own. For a change, as much as is possible, walk away from an argument rather than inviting one. Become more of a peacemaker.

Dropping Your Guard

From God's Vantage Point

You scrutinize my path and my lying down,
and are intimately acquainted
with all my ways.

For Christmas one year we bought our children what was called "Ant City." This consisted of clear plastic plates on either side, filled with sand and ants. From our vantage point outside and above, we could see what these busy little creatures were doing underground. We watched as they tunneled their way around, leaving a maze of trails.

In a similar fashion, God scrutinizes our paths. From where we are, tunneling along, all we see is the sand immediately ahead, behind, and beside us. But from His vantage point, He can see exactly where we've been and precisely where we're going. "He is intimately acquainted with all my ways."

The Mystery of God's Will

Confident Contentment

Teach me to do Your will,
for You are my God;
let Your good Spirit lead
me on level ground.

PSALM 143:10

When Christ becomes our central focus—our reason for existence—contentment replaces our anxiety as well as our fears and insecurities. This cannot help but impact three of the most prevalent joy stealers in all of life.

1. *He broadens the dimensions of our circumstances.* This gives us new confidence. . . .

2. *He delivers us from preoccupation with others.* This causes our contentment level to rise. . . .

3. *He calms our fears regarding ourselves and our future.* This provides a burst of fresh hope on a daily basis.

Laugh Again

Helping the World on to God

Let your light shine before men in such a way that they may see your good works, and glorify your Father who is in heaven.

MATTHEW 5:16

[The world] will see "your good works," Jesus said. Like what?

They will hear your courtesy.

They will detect your smile.

They will notice that you stop to thank them.

They will hear you apologize when you are wrong.

They will see you help them when they are struggling.

They will notice that you are the one who stopped along the road and gave them a hand.

They will see every visible manifestation of Christ's life being normally lived out through you. They will see all that and they "will glorify your Father who is in heaven" (Matt. 5:16). . . .

We are the ones who help the world on to God.

Simple Faith

Absolute Silence

He will exult over you with joy,
He will be quiet in His love.

ZEPHANIAH 3:17

❧ I am more convinced than ever that there is no way you and I can move toward a deeper, intimate relationship with our God without protracted times of stillness, which includes one of the rarest of all experiences: absolute silence.

Am I sounding more like a mystical dreamer? If so, so was the psalmist who wrote those familiar words we often quote but seldom obey, "Be still and know that I am God" (Ps. 46:10, NIV). . . .

We are commanded to stop (literally) . . . rest, relax, let go, and make time for Him. The scene is one of stillness and quietness, listening and waiting before Him. Such foreign experiences in these busy times! Nevertheless, knowing God deeply and intimately requires such discipline. Silence is indispensable if we hope to add depth to our spiritual life.

Intimacy with the Almighty

Faith or Presumption?

We would not trust in ourselves,
but in God . . . [who] will deliver us,
He on whom we have set our hope.

2 CORINTHIANS 1:9–10

The old motto of soldiers during the Revolutionary War applies to many areas of life: "Trust in God, but keep your powder dry!" In other words, place your life in the Savior's hands, but stay at the ready. Do all that you can to prepare yourself for battle, understanding that the ultimate outcome rests with the Lord God.

To walk by faith does not mean stop *thinking*. To trust God does not imply becoming slovenly or lazy or apathetic. . . . You and I need to trust God for our finances, but that is no license to spend foolishly. You and I ought to trust God for safety in the car, but we're not wise to pass on a blind curve. . . .

Acting foolishly or thoughtlessly, expecting God to bail you out if things go amiss, isn't faith at all. It is presumption. Wisdom says, do all you can within your strength, then trust Him to do what you cannot do.

Moses: A Man of Selfless Dedication

The One Thing
We Can Change

> *A wise man is strong,*
> *and a man of knowledge*
> *increases power.*
>
> Proverbs 24:5

This may shock you, but I believe the single most significant decision I can make on a day-to-day basis is my choice of attitude. It is more important than my past, my education, my bankroll, my successes or failures, fame or pain, what other people think of me, or say about me, my circumstances, or my position. The attitude I choose keeps me going or cripples my progress. It alone fuels my fire or assaults my hope. When my attitudes are right, there's no barrier too high, no valley too deep, no dream too extreme, no challenge too great for me.

Yet we must admit that we spend more of our time concentrating and fretting over the things that can't be changed than we do giving attention to the one that we can change— —our choice of attitude.

Day by Day with Charles Swindoll

Seek Righteousness

*Seek first His kingdom
and His righteousness; and all
these things shall be added to you.*

MATTHEW 6:33

🌿 Life is a lot like a coin; you can spend it any way you wish, but you can spend it only once. Choosing one thing over all the rest throughout life is a difficult thing to do. This is especially true when the choices are so many and the possibilities are so close at hand.

To be completely truthful with you, however, we aren't left with numerous possibilities. Jesus Himself gave us the top priority: "Seek first His kingdom and His righteousness." . . .

If I am to seek first in my life God's kingdom and God's righteousness, then whatever else I do ought to relate to that goal: where I work, with whom I spend my time, the one I marry, or the decision to remain single. Every decision I make ought to be filtered through the Matthew 6:33 filter.

Living Above the Level of Mediocrity

Two Key Attitudes

> *Godliness actually is a means*
> *of great gain when accompanied*
> *by contentment.*
>
> 1 TIMOTHY 6:6

🌿 Contentment is something we must learn. It isn't a trait we're born with. But the question is *how?* In 1 Timothy 6 we find a couple of very practical answers to that question:

A current perspective on eternity: "For we have brought nothing into the world, so we cannot take anything out of it either" (v. 7).

A simple acceptance of essentials: "And if we have food and covering, with these we shall be content" (v. 8).

Both attitudes work beautifully. . . . But society's plan of attack is to create dissatisfaction, to convince us that we must be in a constant pursuit for something "out there" that is sure to bring us happiness. . . . It says that contentment is impossible without striving for more,

God's Word offers the exact opposite advice: Contentment is possible when we *stop* striving for more. Contentment never comes from externals. Never!

The Finishing Touch

Amazing Grace

> *Fix your hope completely*
> *on the grace to be brought to you*
> *at the revelation of Jesus Christ.*
>
> 1 PETER 1:13

❧ Imagine coming to the house of a friend who has invited you over to enjoy a meal. You finish the delicious meal and then listen to some fine music and visit for a while. Finally, you stand up and get your coat as you prepare to leave. But before you leave you reach into your pocket and say, "Now, how much do I owe you?" What an insult! You don't do that with someone who has graciously given you a meal.

Isn't it strange, though, how this world is running over with people who think there's something they must do to pay God back? Somehow they are hoping God will smile on them if they work real hard and earn His acceptance. But that's an acceptance on the basis of works. That's not the way it is with grace. . . .

God smiles on us because of His Son's death and resurrection. It's grace, my friend, amazing grace.

The Grace Awakening

If Only . . .

A Cheerful heart has a continual feast.

PROVERBS 15:15

Many folks eat their hearts out, suffering from the contagious "If Only" disease. Its germs infect every slice of life.

> If only I had more money.
> If only we owned a nicer home.
> If only we could have children.
> If only he would ask me out.
> If only I had more friends.

The list is endless. Woven through the fabric of all those words is a sigh that comes from the daily grind of discontentment. Taken far enough, it leads to the dead-end street of self-pity—one of the most distasteful and inexcusable of all attitudes. Discontentment is one of those daily grinds that forces others to listen to our list of woes. But they don't for long! Discontented souls soon become lonely souls.

Living Beyond the Daily Grind

One Day at a Time

When pride comes, then comes dishonor,
but with the humble is wisdom.

People who refuse to get bogged down in and anchored to the past are those who pursue the objectives of the future. People who do this are seldom petty. They are too involved in getting a job done to be occupied with yesterday's hurts and concerns. . . .

I know human nature well enough to realize that some people excuse their bitterness over past hurts by thinking, "It's too late to change. I've been injured and the wrong done against me is too great for me ever to forget it."

But when God holds out hope, when God makes promises, then God says, "It can be done." With each new dawn there is delivered to you door a fresh, new package called "today." God has designed us in such a way that we can handle only one package at a time . . . and all the grace we need will be supplied by Him as we live out that day.

Improving Your Serve

Hope Is More than Dreaming

The way of the LORD
is a stronghold to the upright. . . .
The righteous will never be shaken.

PROVERBS 10:29–30

We toss around words like *faith* and *love* all the time. And most of us can describe both with minimal difficulty. But *hope?* What in the world is it? And is it really *that* essential?

Webster defines hope, "to desire with expectation of fulfillment." To hope is to anticipate. It is more than dreaming, however. It is possessing within ourselves an expectation that someday there will be the fulfillment of that desire. It will become a reality. Hope always looks to the future, it's always on tiptoes. It keeps us going. It makes a dismal today bearable because it promises a brighter tomorrow. Without hope, something inside all of us dies. . . .

We can live several weeks without food, days without water, and only minutes without oxygen, but without hope—forget it.

Dropping Your Guard

Wisdom

*Strength is more impressive
yet less effective than wisdom.*

Perfect Trust

*The LORD also will be
a stronghold for the oppressed,
a stronghold in times of trouble.*

PSALM 9:9

When the Philistines seized David in Gath he said "When I am afraid, I will put my trust in You." (Psalm 56:3). When he fled from Saul into a cave, he cried out to God. "My soul takes refuge in You; and in the shadow of Your wings I will take refuge until destruction passes by" (Psalm 57:1).

Many, many years ago, Felix of Nola was escaping his enemies, and he, too, took temporary refuge in a cave. He had scarcely entered the opening of the cave before a spider began to weave its web across the small opening. With remarkable speed, the insect completely sealed off the mouth of the cave with an intricate web, giving the appearance that the cave had not been entered for many weeks. As Felix's pursuers passed by, they saw the web and didn't even bother to look inside. Later, as the godly fugitive stepped out into the sunlight, he uttered these insightful words: "Where God is, a spider's web is a wall; where He is not, a wall is but a spider's web."

Perfect Trust

The Great Gift of Fidelity

A faithful man will abound with blessings.

PROVERBS 28:20

🌺 We are living in an era that attempts to stretch grace to heretical extremes. I see it and hear it virtually every week of my life. So allow me to say this very straight: The greatest gift you can give to your marriage partner is your purity, your fidelity. The greatest character trait you can provide your spouse and your family is moral and ethical self-control. Stand firm, my friend. Refuse to yield [to temptation].

Deceptive baits are set out about us each day, and they don't all come from individuals. Some of them come from a cable television channel or the Internet or a magazine or peer pressure at school or colleagues at work. . . . You'll feel like a prude, the only one around who's not yielding. Don't be deceived by the persuasion no matter how beautiful and appealing the words may sound. It is a lie. Remember, it is all a lie.

Joseph: A Man of Integrity and Forgiveness

God Is There, Every Hour

Do not fear, for I am with you;
do not anxiously look about you,
for I am your God.

Back in World War II a scribble of comic graffiti began appearing on walls everywhere, proclaiming, "Kilroy was here!" This declaration was found on walls in Germany. It was found on buildings in Tokyo. It was found on big boulders in America. Kilroy was *everywhere,* it seemed.

God is not like Kilroy. He does not write His name on the walls and rocks of life, but He is there—every day, every hour, every tick of the clock! To borrow the now-classic words of the late Francis Schaeffer, "He is there and He is not silent." Never doubt the presence of God.

He is there with you on your own personal pilgrimage . . . His unsearchable mind working in concert with His unfathomable will, carrying things out under His sovereign control.

Esther: A Woman of Strength and Dignity

A Present Help

The LORD of hosts is with us;
the God of Jacob is our stronghold.

PSALM 46:7

We deny it. We fake it. We mask it. We try to ignore it. But the truth, stubbornly persists—we are *weak* creatures! Being sinful, we fail. Being prone to sickness, we hurt. Being mortal, we ultimately die. Pressure wears on us. Anxiety gives us ulcers. People intimidate us. Criticism offends us. Disease scares us. Death haunts us. . . .

How can we continue to grow in this bag of bones, covered with weaknesses too numerous to mention? We need a big dose of Psalm 46: "God is our refuge and strength, a very present help in trouble." What hope for those struggling through the grind of personal weaknesses!

Living Beyond the Daily Grind

God Is in Charge

I have composed and quieted my soul;
like a weaned child rests against his mother,
my soul is like a weaned child within me.

When it comes to irritations, I've found that it helps if I remember that I am not in charge of my day . . . God is. And while I'm sure He wants me to use my time wisely, He is more concerned with the development of my character and the cultivation of the qualities that make me Christ-like within. One of His preferred methods of training is through adjustments to irritations.

A perfect illustration? The oyster and its pearl.

Irritation occurs when the shell of the oyster is invaded by an alien substance like a grain of sand. When that happens, all the resources within the tiny, sensitive oyster rush to the irritated spot and begin to release healing fluids that otherwise would have remained dormant. By and by the irritant is covered—by a pearl. Had there been no irritating interruption, there could have been no pearl.

No wonder our heavenly home has pearly gates to welcome the wounded and bruised who have responded correctly to the sting of irritations.

The Finishing Touch

Keep to the Quest

Acquire wisdom!
Acquire understanding!
Do not forget nor turn away
from the words of my mouth.

PROVERBS 4:5

All of us are surrounded by and benefit from the results of someone's quest. Let me name a few:

Above my head is a bright electric light. Thanks, Tom.

On my nose are eyeglasses that enable me to focus. Thanks, Ben.

In my driveway is a car ready to take me wherever I choose to steer it. Thanks, Henry.

Across my shelves are books full of interesting and carefully researched pages. Thanks, authors.

My list could go on and on. So could yours.

Because some cared enough to dream, to pursue, to follow through and complete their quest, our lives are more comfortable, more stable.

That's enough to spur me on. How about you?

Day by Day with Charles Swindoll

Big-Picture Perspective

You are my hiding place
and my shield;
I wait for Your word.

PSALM 119:114

One of the greatest benefits to be gleaned from the Bible is perspective. When we get discouraged, we temporarily lose our perspective. Little things become mammoth. A slight irritation, such as a pebble in a shoe, seems huge. Motivation is drained away and, worst of all, hope departs.

God's Word is tailor-made for gray-slush days. It sends a beam of light through the fog. It signals safety when we fear we'll never make it through. Such big-picture perspective gives us a hope transplant, and within a brief period of time, we have escaped the bleak and boring and we're back at soaring. . . .

We can actually stand firm through discouraging times but only if we apply God's instructions.

Living Above the Level of Mediocrity

Glorify God
to the Maximum

I will give thanks to you, O Lord,
among the peoples, and I will sing
praises to You among the nations.

Psalm 108:3

By making us in His image, God gave us capacities not given to other forms of life. Ideally, He made us to know Him, to love Him, and to obey Him. He did not put rings in our noses that He might pull us around like oxen. . . .

No, He gave us freedom to make choices. By His grace we are equipped to understand His plan because we have a mind with which we can know Him. We are also free to love and adore Him because we have emotions. He takes pleasure in our affection and devotion. We can obey His instructions but we are not pawns on a global chessboard. It is in the voluntary spontaneity of our response that He finds divine pleasure. When His people freely respond in worship and praise, obedience and adoration, God is glorified to the maximum.

Laugh Again

We Weep and Pray, Grow and Learn

Man's steps are ordained by the LORD, how then can man understand his way?

PROVERBS 20:24

Tests are never wasted. God never says, "Oops, made a mistake on that one. I shouldn't have given you that. I meant that for Frank. Sorry, Bob." It's as if the Lord has our name on specific trials. They are specifically designed for us, arranged with our weaknesses and our immaturity in mind. He bears down and doesn't let up. And we groan and we hurt and we weep and we pray and we grow and we learn. Through it all we learn to depend upon His Word. . . .

The common response to trials is resistance, if not outright resentment. How much better that we open the doors of our hearts and welcome the God-ordained trials as honored guests for the good they do in our lives.

Hope Again

Understanding
and Obedience

> *The Lord GOD has opened My ear;*
> *and I was not disobedient*
> *nor did I turn back.*
>
> ISAIAH 50:5

🌿 Our greatest struggle is not in the realm of understanding the will of God; it's in the realm of *obeying* the God whose will it is. To be painfully honest, when you and I look back at our lives, we do not find ourselves puzzled and mystified about God's will nearly as much as we find ourselves stubborn and resistant to the One directing our steps. Our problem isn't that we don't know; our problem is that we *do* know but aren't willing to follow through.

That's the basic struggle of the Christian life. The clear truth of God is set before us time and time again. It's available to us, we read it, we hear it explained from the pulpit, in a Christian book, or on a Christian radio program, and we sense the Holy Spirit whispering, *Yes, this means you.* We understand Him clearly, but we resist. When the chips are down, our tendency is to say, "I've got it planned another way."

Moses: A Man of Selfless Dedication

Life in Living Color

I love Your commandments above gold,
yes, above fine gold. Therefore I esteem right
all Your precepts concerning everything.

PSALM 119:127–128

The thing I have always appreciated about the Bible is that when great truth is given, God frequently incarnates that truth in lives with whom we can identify. He doesn't stop at theory as He teaches us about the abstract importance of faith. He mentions Abraham as a model "who staggered not at the promise of God through unbelief."

He doesn't just talk about standing alone and being people of character and resiliency—He gives us Elijah. He shows us the prophets because we have much greater difficulty identifying with abstract truth. We can, however, identify with people. . . .

God doesn't just say, "You ought to forgiven." He gives us Joseph, who forgave his brothers for their mistreatment of him. God paints His heroes "warts and all." Since there are scars and a dark side to every life, we're not shielded from the Jonahs and the Samsons, from the pride of the King Sauls or the adultery of the King Davids. We see it in raw, living color.

Living on the Ragged Edge

A Sweet, Winsome Melody

Whatever is true, whatever is honorable,
whatever is right, whatever is pure,
whatever is lovely, whatever is of good
repute . . . dwell on these things.

Let me urge you to take charge of your mind and emotions today. Let your mind feast on nutritious food for a change. Refuse to grumble and criticize! Let your life yield a sweet, winsome melody that this old world needs so desperately. Fix your attention on these six specifics in life:

Not unreal far-fetched dreams, but things that are true . . .

Not cheap, flippant, superficial stuff, but things that are honorable . . .

Not things that are wrong and unjust, . . . but that which is right.

Not thoughts that are carnal, smutty, and obscene, but that which is pure . . .

Not things that prompt arguments and defense in others, but those that are agreeable, . . .

Not slander, gossip, and put-downs, but information of good report, the kind that builds up and causes grace to flow.

Strengthening Your Grip

WISDOM FOR THE WAY   91

Enduring Faith

Let endurance have its perfect result,
that you may be perfect and complete,
lacking in nothing.

JAMES 1:4

We're very fickle in our faith, aren't we? We are inconsistent, ambivalent. We sing *"My faith looks up to Thee"* . . . until the medicine stops working, until the lights go out, until the bill comes due and we don't have what it takes to pay it. Until our grades slip or our career takes a turn or we loose a mate. . . .

How do we learn consistent faith? We learn it one day at a time. We learn it through *endurance*. James writes: "Consider it all joy, my brethren, when you encounter various trials, knowing that the testing of your faith produces endurance" (James 1:2–3). He's not talking about a will-o'-the-wisp faith that starts out on the 100-meter sprint and, quicker than you can think, is over. Anybody can handle that kind of faith. Anybody can take ten, fifteen, or twenty minutes of a test. But ten days or fifteen days, or a year, or two or three? Well, that's another matter. That's the enduring faith James is talking about.

Perfect Trust

A Proper Perspective

> *So therefore, no one of you can be My disciple*
> *who does not give up all his own possessions.*
>
> LUKE 14:33

❀ Jesus' words are neither complicated nor vague. He simply says, "If you are going to call yourself one of My disciples, you must release your grip on materialism." To keep all this in proper perspective, think of it this way. He is not saying that we cannot posses anything, but things must not be allowed to possess us. To use His words, we must "give up" our possessions.

Corrie ten Boom, that saintly lady who endured such brutality from the Nazis in Ravensbruck during World War II, once said that she had learned to hold everything loosely in her hand. She said she discovered, in her years of walking with Him, that when she grasped things tightly, it would hurt when the Lord would have to pry her fingers loose. Disciples hold all "things" loosely.

Do you? Can you think of *anything* that has a tap root to your heart? Let go! Give it up to Him! Yes, it may be painful. . . but how essential!

Strengthening Your Grip

Claim God's Grace

For by grace you have been saved
through faith; and that not of yourselves,
it is the gift of God

EPHESIANS 2:8

While most people in the world are busy building towers with highest hopes of making a name and gaining fame, God's truth sets the record straight. On the basis of God's Book, His Holy Word, it is my plea that we simply admit our need and claim God's grace. Instead of striving for a manmade ticket to heaven based on high achievement and hard work (for which *we* get all the credit), I suggest we openly declare our own spiritual bankruptcy and accept God's free gift of grace. "Why?" you ask. "Why not emphasize how much I do for God instead of what He does for me?" Because that is heresy, plain and simple. How? By exalting my own effort and striving for my own accomplishments, I insult His grace and steal credit that belongs to Him only.

The Grace Awakening

The Riddles of Life

By His breath the heavens are cleared,
His hand has pierced the fleeing serpent. . . .
But His mighty thunder, who can understand?

There are numerous riddles in life that remain wrapped in mystery and shrouded inside an enigma. The sea, for example, is an unexplainable phenomenon. Who can fathom its tide affected strangely by the moon . . . ?

We manage to continue on, though brilliant scientists have been trying to solve and/or explain life's mysteries for years. . . . But when God leaves us with a mystery that isn't solved in a week or two, most of us go through desperate struggles believing that He is good or fair. I mean, after all, if we're going to trust a good God, He should do only good things, right? No fair doing mysterious stuff!

The Bible that I read simply doesn't present that as the way life is. Yet the world I live in seems to expect that. And that's certainly the cynic's line: "You mean to tell my you are going to trust a God who treats you like that?" When will we ever learn that cynics have no capacity to understand the profound and unfathomable ways of God?

Living on the Ragged Edge

Serving Is Essential

Through love serve one another.

GALATIANS 5:13

Our world has become a large, impersonal, busy institution. We are alienated from each other. Although crowded, we are lonely. Distant. Pushed together but uninvolved. No longer do most neighbors visit across the backyard fence. The well-manicured front lawn is the modern moat that keeps barbarians at bay. Hoarding and flaunting have replaced sharing and caring. It's like we are occupying common space but have no common interests, as if we're on an elevator with rules like: "No talking, smiling, or eye contact allowed without written consent of the management."

Painful though it may be for us to admit it here in this great land of America, we're losing touch with one another. The motivation to help, to encourage, yes, to serve our fellow-man is waning. . . . And yet, it is these things that form the essentials of a happy and fulfilled life.

Improving Your Serve

God Is Awesome!

Be exalted, O God, above the heavens,
and Your glory above all the earth.

When was the last time you took a glance at a mountain? You don't glance at pictures of Mount Everest and say, " Hmm, nice hill. Maybe a little taller than some mountains." You don't witness the glaciers in Alaska and say, "Oh, yeah, that's a pretty nice glacier." You stand in silent awe.

I remember when my Marine battalion flew over Japan's Mount Fuji. Not one man on our plane, when they looked out and saw Fuji, said, "Sure, sure, that's nice," No, indeed! I mean, it was click, click, click . . . it was picture taking time! *This* was picturesque, awesome Fuji!

Who made Fuji? God! And like that mountain, the rest of His creation is equally awesome. Consider the stars in space, for example. Though we were to study for a lifetime, we still could not fathom them. When God does it, it makes us stand back in respect. It puts all human achievements on the lowest level.

Living on the Ragged Edge

Worry Is Distracting

Be anxious for nothing, but in everything
by prayer and supplication with thanksgiving
let your requests be made known to God.

PHILIPPIANS 4:6

Anxious. Intriguing word. It literally means "to be divided" or "distracted." . . .

We find a perfect illustration of this in the story of Mary and Martha recorded in Luke 10:38–42. Taking a minute to look into their little abode, we find that Martha is distracted, *anxious.* Jesus is sitting down talking, and Mary is sitting at His feet, enjoying His presence, . . . and His teachings. But not Martha. She is busy back in the kitchen getting everything ready for a big meal. In good womanly fashion she is making everything match, everything fit, everything come out of the oven at just the right time. . . .

But Jesus wanted her to come and sit down beside her sister and listen. It wasn't that He didn't appreciate her efforts. He just wanted her to serve a simple dish so they could make the most of their time together. . . . Her anxiety was distracting her from more important things. Worry always does that.

Perfect Trust

No Mass-Produced Saints

Know that the LORD Himself is God;
it is He who made us, and not we ourselves.

PSALM 100:3

We live today in a microwave culture. If it takes longer than five minutes to fix lunch, that's long! In earlier days, you even had to wait for a TV set to warm up. Can you imagine? And you couldn't push a single button on your phone to call home on a pre-set number, you had to *dial* it . . . with your finger, for pity's sake. Talk about the stone age! I remember driving by a vacant lot some time ago, then going by the same corner several weeks later. Where there had been nothing but grass and weeds, empty beer cans, and trash just days before, there was now a huge warehouse, assembled from pre-fab sections, ready to receive goods.

That's the way life is today. Fast. Compressed. Condensed. Slam-bang-it's-done. Not so in God's wilderness schooling. When it comes to walking with God, there is no such thing as instant maturity. God doesn't mass produce His saints. He hand-tools each one, and it always takes longer than we expected.

Moses: A Man of Selfless Dedication

God in Our Conversation

*You shall teach [God's commands]
diligently to your sons and shall talk
of them when you sit in your house.*

DEUTERONOMY 6:7

We are to talk of spiritual things in our homes just as we would talk about anything else. You talk together about how the Dodgers played last night. No big deal, you just talk about that. You talk about what you're going to do next week. You don't lecture on it. You don't make a big announcement, you simply talk about it. . . . You may talk about what you plan to watch on television that evening. You don't hold classes on it, you merely talk about it. There is an easygoing, natural flow of conversation. . . .

That is what will make your Christianity authentic. It isn't a Sunday lifestyle! It's a Monday, Tuesday, Wednesday, Thursday, Friday, Saturday, and Sunday cycle-of-living lifestyle. So much so, that Christ fits naturally into the regular conversation of the home.

Growing Wise in Family Life

Considering Quitting?

> *Come to Me, all who are weary*
> *and heavy-laden, and I will give you rest . . .*
> *for My yoke is easy and My burden is light.*
>
> MATTHEW 11:28, 30

❧ Every achievement worth remembering is stained with the blood of diligence and scarred by the wounds of disappointment. To quit, to run, to escape, to hide—none of these options solve anything. They only postpone the acceptance of, and reckoning with, reality.

Churchill put it well: "Wars are not won by evacuations." . . .

Giving thought to giving up?

Considering the possibility of quitting? . . .

Don't! . . . The only time the Lord ever used the word "easy" was when He referred to a yoke.

Day by Day with Charles Swindoll

Stand Tall, Stand Firm

Your God has commanded your strength.

PSALM 68:28

Today there are those who stand alone in the gap, those who still strive to shake us awake. A handful of brave students at Columbine High School come immediately to mind. Loaded guns and the threat of death couldn't silence them. I think of them a modern-day [prophets], whom God uses to deliver a life-changing message. Men and women of courage, ready to stand and deliver. Authentic heroes. . . .

Our Lord is still searching for people who will make a difference. Christians dare not be mediocre. We dare not dissolve into the background or blend into the neutral scenery of this world. . . .

In our culture—our schools, our offices and factories, our lunchrooms and boardrooms, our halls of ivy and our halls of justice—we need men and women of God, young people of God. We need respected professionals, athletes, homemakers, teachers, public figures, and private citizens who will promote the things of God, who will stand alone—stand tall, stand firm, stand strong!

Elijah: A Man of Heroism & Humility

Invincible, Immutable, and Infinite

Now to the King eternal,
immortal, invisible, the only God,
be honor and glory forever and ever.

1 TIMOTHY 1:17

Whoever is sovereign must have total, clear perspective. He must see the end from the beginning. He must have no match on earth or in heaven. He must entertain no fears, no ignorance, and have no needs. He must have no limitations and always know what is best. He must never make a mistake. He must possess the ability to bring everything to a purposeful conclusion and an ultimate goal. He must be invincible, immutable, infinite, and self-sufficient. His judgments must be unsearchable and His ways unfathomable. He must be able to create rather than invent, to direct rather than wish, to control rather than hope, to guide rather than guess, to fulfill rather than dream.

Who qualifies? You guessed it . . . God, and God alone.

The Mystery of God's Will

Let God Do the Exalting

When a man's ways are
pleasing to the LORD, He makes even
his enemies to be at peace with him.

Think of David, the young musician, tending his father's sheep back on the hills of Judea many centuries ago. He was a self-taught, gifted musician. He didn't go on tour, trying to make a name for himself. Instead, he sang to the sheep. He had no idea that someday his lyrics would find their way into the psalter or would be the very songs that have inspired and comforted millions of people through long and dark nights.

David didn't seek success; he simply humbled himself under the mighty hand of God, staying close to the Lord and submitting himself to Him. And God exalted David to the highest position in the land. . . .

You don't have to promote yourself. . . . God will promote you. . . . Let God do the exalting! In the meantime, sit quietly under His hand.

Hope Again

A Deliberate Trust

> *In you, O LORD,*
> *I have taken refuge.*
>
> PSALM 31:1

Under heaven's lock and key, we are protected by the most efficient security system available—the power of God. There is no way we will be lost in the process of suffering. No disorder, no disease, not even death itself can weak or threaten God's ultimate protection over our lives. . . .

"God stands between you and all that menaces your hope or threatens your eternal welfare," James Moffatt wrote. "The protection here is entirely and directly the work of God."

Two words will help you cope when you run low on hope: *accept* and *trust*.

Accept the mystery of hardship, suffering, misfortune, or mistreatment. Don't try to understand it or explain it. Accept it. Then, deliberately *trust* God to protect you by His power from this very moment to the dawning of eternity.

Hope Again

Care and Concern
for Others

> *Clothe yourselves with humility*
> *toward one another, for God is opposed to the*
> *proud, but gives grace to the humble.*
>
> 1 PETER 5:5

Humility of mind is really an attitude, isn't it? It's a preset mentality that determines ahead of time thoughts like this:

I care about those around me.

Why do I always have to be first?

I'm going to help someone else win for a change.

Today I'm going to curb my fierce competitive tendencies.

Instead of always thinking about receiving, we'll start looking for ways to give. Instead of holding grudges against those who offend us, we'll be anxious to forgive. And instead of keeping a record of what we've done or who we've helped, we'll take delight in forgetting the deed(s) and being virtually unnoticed. Our hunger for public recognition will diminish in significance.

Improving Your Serve

Living a Holy Life

Consecrate yourselves therefore,
and be holy, for I am holy.

LEVITICUS 11:44

As Christians we live a life that is different—morally excellent, ethically beautiful. It's called a holy life. And God honors that. Because it's like He is. . . .

All of our Christian lives we have sung the old hymn "Take Time to Be Holy." Those words are true. It does take time to be holy. It certainly takes time to be mature. It takes time to cultivate a walk with the Lord that begins to flow naturally because the enemy is so much more assertive and powerful than we . . . and so creative, so full of new ideas on how to derail us and demoralize us.

We need to lock onto the power that comes from God's presence and invite Him to cleanse our thoughts, to correct our foul speech, to forgive us completely, and make us holy vessels, who, like the winged seraphim, spend our days bringing glory to His holy name.

Day by Day with Charles Swindoll

No Place for Pride

It is better to be humble in spirit
with the lowly than to divide the spoil
with the proud.

PROVERBS 16:19

Someone who is truly unselfish is generous with his or her time and possessions, energy and money. As that works its way out, it is demonstrated in various ways, such as thoughtfulness and gentleness, an unpretentious spirit, and servant-hearted leadership.

When a husband is unselfish, he subjugates his own wants and desires to the needs of his wife and family.

When a mother is unselfish, she isn't irked by having to give up her agenda or plans for the sake of her children.

When an athlete is unselfish, it is the team that matters, not winning the top honors personally.

When a Christian is unselfish, others mean more than self. Pride is given no place to operate.

Laugh Again

God's Topsy-Turvy Ways

> *How unsearchable are His judgments*
> *and unfathomable His ways!*
>
> HEBREWS 11:33

🌸 God's ways are topsy-turvy to the world's ways. A few examples: God exalts the humble, but the world exalts the proud. God ascribes greatness, not to masters, but to servants. God is impressed, not with noise or size or wealth, but with quiet things . . . done in secret—the inner motives, the true heart condition. God sends away the arrogant and the rich empty-handed, but He gathers to Himself the lowly, the broken, the prisoner, the prostitute, the repentant. The world honors the handsome and the gifted and the brilliant. God smiles on the crippled, the ones who can't keep up. All this makes the world nervous.

As Dietrich Bonhoeffer wrote in *The Cost of Discipleship*: "And so the disciples are strangers in the world, unwelcome guests, disturbers of the peace. No wonder the world rejects them!"

Simple Faith

God Speaks to the Quiet Heart

*A day in Your courts is
better than a thousand outside.*

PSALM 84:2, 10

❧ If the pace and the push, the noise and the crowds are getting to you, it's time to stop the nonsense and find a place of solace to refresh your spirit. Deliberately say "no" more often. This will leave room for you to slow down, get alone, pour out your overburdened heart, and admit your desperate need for inner refreshment. The good news is God will hear and He will help. The bad news is this: If you wait for someone else to bring about a change, things will only deteriorate.

All of us can testify, God does not speak to the hurried, worried mind. It takes time alone with Him and His Word before we can expect our spiritual strength to recover.

Intimacy with the Almighty

Wisdom

Wisdom gives us balance, strength,
and insight. None of these is a natural trait;
each is a by-product of wisdom.

A Giant Step
Toward Maturity

My flesh and my heart may fail,
but God is the strength of my heart
and my portion forever.

One of the hardest things for you and me to do is own up to our own failures. Whether we're talking to our spouses, our kids, our employers, or with our Lord Himself, it goes against the grain to come clean and admit our offenses. The knee-jerk response every time is to employ defense mechanisms: to deny, to excuse, to rationalize, to *reinterpret* our shortfalls.

The best and healthiest course is to 'fess up. To call failure, "failure." To name sin for what it is. To admit we were wrong, and having declared it, to learn what God may have to teach us from the experience.

Sir Winston Churchill . . . offered the best definition of success I've ever read: "Success is moving from one failure to another with no loss of enthusiasm." . . . As you begin to interpret failure correctly, you will take your first giant step toward maturity.

Moses: A Man of Selfless Dedication

Sow Generously,
Reap Generously

Bless the LORD, O my soul,
and forget none of His benefits.

PSALM 103:1

🌿 Do you have eyesight? It's a gift. Do you have a good mind? It's a gift. Do you have leadership abilities that cause others to follow? A good education? These are all gifts. Has God given you a family? Has He given you sufficient clothes? . . . These are all gifts from God's hand. Reflect on His numerous gifts to you. It will increase your joy. . . .

Then remind yourself of God's promises regarding generosity. God promises if you sow bountifully, you will reap bountifully. So give! Give abundantly! Even extravagant giving is honored by God. I've never known anyone who went bad because he or she was too generous. Remind yourself of His promises regarding generosity and start giving!

Don't be afraid of out-giving God. It is absolutely impossible to do that.

Living Above the Level of Mediocrity

Seeking Success

*When pride comes,
then comes dishonor, but with
the humble is wisdom.*

PROVERBS 11:2

We are a success-saturated society. The tell-tale signs are everywhere. Each year dozens of books and magazines, scores of audio and video tapes, and hundreds of seminars offer ideas, motivation, techniques, and promises of prosperity.

Curiously, however, few ever address what it is most folks want (but seldom find) in their pursuit of success: contentment, fulfillment, satisfaction, and relief. . . .

At the risk of sounding ultra-simplistic, I'd like to offer some counsel to those seeking success. . . .

First, submit yourself to those who are wise. . . .

Second, humble yourself under God's mighty hand. . . .

Third, throw yourself on the mercy and care of God.

The Finishing Touch

Magnificent Relief

I acknowledged my sin to You . . .
and You forgave the guilt of my sin.

PSALM 32:5

🌿 Like a cool, cleansing shower on a hot, sweaty day, God's forgiveness washes away not only sins but their tormenting guilt. God goes into the depths of our inner being and provides that magnificent relief that only He can bring: PEACE. . . .

If you are harboring some sin—if you are keeping hidden a few secret regions of wrong—don't expect to enjoy freedom from guilt, child of God. There is an unspoken axiom threaded through Scripture: secret sin cannot coexist with inner peace. Peace returns only when our sins are fully confessed and forsaken. Few grinds are more galling than the grind of an unforgiven conscience. It's awful! And few joys are more relieving than having our sins forgiven. It's wonderful!

Living Beyond the Daily Grind

What to Do with Worry

Do not worry about tomorrow;
for tomorrow will care for itself. Each day
has enough trouble of its own.

MATTHEW 6:34

❧ Here's a question worth your time: What are we to do when worry comes knocking on the door of our mind? First, we must set our minds on Christ. "Seek first His kingdom and His righteousness; and all these things [that would worry you] shall be added to you" (Matthew 6:33). When the temptation to worry first arrives, that's the critical moment. The tendency is to entertain it. To let it onto the front porch and allow it to sit there. But before you know it, worry has crawled in through the window and made itself at home! No, worry must be stopped. We have to decide that we are going to commit this worry to God right now and refuse to entertain it, even on the front porch of our thinking.

Perfect Trust

Meaningful Memorials

So these days were to be remembered
and celebrated throughout every generation,
every family, every province, and every city.

ESTHER 9:28

❧ The Lincoln Memorial. The Vietnam Memorial. . . . Memorials are places provided for us to stand and be quiet, to reflect, and to pass on to the next generation the roots of a nation's heritage. They give the present significance because they give the past perspective.

My fear for our present rapid-paced lifestyle is that we have so few memorials, so few monuments, even mental monuments. Life is lived in the fast lane. Superficial decisions. Hurry-up childhoods. . . . So little time spent stopping and recording segments of our lives in a journal. So little emphasis on listening and learning and honoring. . . .

In order to have perspective, we must have monuments and memorials, places to return to and learn from and talk about and pass on. If we don't, we are destined to live rootless, fast-lane lives without much significance.

Esther: A Woman of Strength and Dignity

Sacred Serendipity

*I will once again deal marvelously
with this people, wondrously marvelous.*

ISAIAH 29:14

🌾 *Seren-dip-ity*—the *dip* of the *serene* into the common responsibilities of life. Serendipity occurs when something beautiful breaks into the monotonous and the mundane. A serendipitous life is marked by "surprisability" and spontaneity. When we lose our capacity for either, we settle into life's ruts. We expect little and we're seldom disappointed.

Though I have walked with God for several decades, I must confess I still find much about Him incomprehensible and mysterious. But this much I know: He delights in surprising us. He dots our pilgrimage from earth to heaven with amazing serendipities. . . . .

Your situation may be as hot and barren as a desert or as forlorn and meaningless as a wasteland. . . . But all I ask is that you . . . be on the lookout. God may very well be planning a serendipity in your life.

The Finishing Touch

Forever Discontented

> *Beware, and be on your guard against*
> *every form of greed; for not even when one has an*
> *abundance does his life consist of his possessions.*

LUKE 12:15

Let's take a brief look at greed. Practically speaking, greed is an inordinate desire for more, an excessive, unsatisfied hunger to possess. Like an untamed beast, greed grasps, claws, reaches, clutches, and clings—stubbornly refusing to surrender. The word *enough* is not in this beast's vocabulary. Akin to envy and jealousy, greed is nevertheless distinct. Envy wants to have what someone else possesses. Jealousy want to possess what it already has. But greed is different. Greed is forever discontented and therefore insatiably craving, longing, wanting, striving for more, more, more. . . .

That's the whole point of greed. You'll want more and more of something that really isn't good for you. And in the getting of it, you'll suffer the painful consequences. That's why Jesus warns, "Beware. Be on your guard. This thing is like a cancer—an insatiable leech that will suck the life right out of you." Enough will never be enough.

Beware.

Living Above the Level of Mediocrity

Outrageous Joy

In your presence is fullness of joy;
in your right hand there are pleasures forever.

PSALM 16:11

🌿 I know of no greater need today than the need for joy. Unexplainable, contagious joy. Outrageous joy.

When that kind of joy comes aboard our ship of life, it brings things with it—like enthusiasm for life, determination to hang in there, and a strong desire to be of encouragement to others. Such qualities make our voyage bearable when we hit the open seas and encounter high waves of hardship that tend to demoralize and paralyze. There is nothing better than a joyful attitude when we face the challenges life throws at us.

Someone once asked Mother Teresa what the job description was for anyone who might wish to work alongside her in the grimy streets and narrow alleys of Calcutta. Without hesitation she mentioned only two things: the desire to work hard and a joyful attitude.

Laugh Again

The Sheltering Tree
of Friendship

A friend loves at all times,
and a brother is born for adversity.

PROVERBS 17:17

The poet Samuel Coleridge once described friendship as "a sheltering tree." When you have this quality, the branches of your friendship reach out over the lives of others, giving them shelter, shade, rest, relief, and encouragement. . . .

Friends give comfort. We find strength near them. They bear fruit that provides nourishment and encouragement. When something troublesome occurs in our life, we pick up the phone and call a friend, needing the comfort he or she provides. I think there are few things more lonely than having no friend to call. Friends also care enough about us to hold us accountable . . . but we never doubt their love or respect.

Hope Again

Priorities for Parents

My son, if your heart is wise,
my own heart also will be glad.

PROVERBS 23:15

Let me make three practical suggestions to you who are parents.

First, *determine your priorities*. Ask yourself how high the family rates on your list of involvement. How are your children in particular—just how serious are you regarding time with each? Have you told them or your mate? . . .

Second, *record your observations*. If a child reveals his or her bents in everyday life, those things are worth writing down. Keep a journal on each child. . . . As you write, pray for wisdom. Ask God to guide your thoughts. Please remember, each child is unique. No comparisons! . . .

Third, *share your findings*. Children long to know themselves better. They respect your counsel, and will long remember your remarks. Be candid and honest as you help them "see" who they really are.

Growing Wise in Family Life

The Impossible Is God's Ideal

> *Do not be afraid. Stand still, and*
> *see the salvation of the LORD, which*
> *He will accomplish for you today.*
>
> EXODUS 14:13, NKJV

I'd like to underline a major truth in this world of ours that I don't pretend to understand. Here it is: The best framework for the Lord God to do His most ideal work is when things are absolutely impossible and we feel totally unqualified to handle it. That's His favorite circumstance. Those are His ideal working conditions.

God does His most magnificent work when the situation seems totally impossible from a human point of view, and we feel absolutely unprepared and unable to do anything about it, *yet our eyes are on Him . . .* That's when God rolls up His big sleeves and says, "Step back out of the way a moment, and watch Me work."

Time after time, He brings us to our absolute end and then proves Himself faithful. That, my friend, is the story of the Bible in a nutshell.

Moses: A Man of Selfless Dedication

A Beautiful Balance

*He who pursues
righteousness and loyalty finds life,
righteousness and honor.*

PROVERBS 21:21

We've been programmed to think that fatigue is next to godliness. That the more exhausted we are (and look!), the more committed we are to spiritual things and the more we earn God's smile of approval. . . . As a result, we have become a generation of people who worship our work . . . who work at our play . . . and who play at our worship.

Hold it! Who wrote that rule? Why have we bought that philosophy? Whatever possessed someone to make such a statement? How did we ever get caught in that maddening undertow?

I challenge you to support it from the Scriptures. Start with the life (and *lifestyle*) of Jesus Christ. . . . His was a life of beautiful balance. He accomplished everything the Father sent Him to do. Everything. And He did it without ignoring those essential times of restful leisure. If that is the way *He* lived, then it makes good sense that that is the way we, too, must learn to live.

Strengthening Your Grip

Heed God's Promptings

The mind of man plans his way,
but the LORD directs his steps.

PROVERBS 16:9

Nothing wrong with planning. Nothing wrong with thinking it through. Nothing wrong with doing your charts, listing all the pros and cons, talking it over. But as you are moving along, stay sensitive to the quiet, yet all-important prompting of God through His Holy Spirit. It's easier to steer a moving car. Just get the car rolling and you can push it into the filling station to get the gas. But it's hard to get it moving from a dead stop. So you're on your way, you're making your plans, you're thinking it through. Just stay open. . . .

As author Henry Blackaby says, "Watch to see where God is at work and join Him!" Just go there. Why do you want to be anywhere God *isn't* at work?

The Mystery of God's Will

Wisdom in the Wilderness

I have directed you in the way of wisdom;
I have led you in upright paths.

PROVERBS 4:11

The Hebrew word for "desert" is *midbaar*. It's from the word *dahbaar*, meaning "to speak." Let me draw from that root term and suggest that the desert is the place where God speaks, where He communicates some of His most important messages to us. . . .

Your desert experience might involve caring for an ailing family member or an elderly parent over an extended time, with no help at hand and no relief in sight. Your sojourn in the dry lands might be a stubborn physical condition that keeps you confined. It could be that deep soul-ache that comes with an unfaithful spouse, or a rebellious teenager. . . .

Does God know? Does He understand? He understands very well, my friend. After all, He's the One who *put* you there. His schooling includes time in the wilderness. That's where He gets our attention.

Moses: A Man of Selfless Dedication

A Worry or Two or Three . . .

And which of you by worrying
can add a single hour to his life's span?

LUKE 12:25

In the depths of every person's soul, in the secret chambers where no one else knows the thoughts, we are usually able to find a worry or two or three. Even in the hearts of those who are laughing and smiling.

We worry about death—our own or that of a loved one. We worry about disobedience and sin, about feelings of guilt. We worry about daily problems—people problems, decision problems, problems related to work, home, relationships, finances, school . . . you name it, we worry about it. . . .

One of the problems with worry is that *it keeps you from enjoying what you have.* When you worry about what you don't have, you won't be able to enjoy what you do have. That's what Jesus was talking about in Matthew 6:25: "I say to you, do not be anxious for your life, as to what you shall eat, or what you shall drink. . . ." Worry is assuming responsibilities that you cannot handle. The truth is, they are responsibilities that God never intended for you to handle, because they are His.

Perfect Trust

God's Truth Incarnated

*The commandment is a lamp
and the teaching is light; and reproofs
for discipline are the way of life.*

❦ The tyranny of the urgent will always out-shout the essential nature of the important . . . if we let it. We have to determine not to let that happen. The secret is establishing personal priorities. I have suggested four:

Set a firm foundation—be *biblical.*

Apply the truth of the Scriptures—be *authentic.*

Develop a compassionate attitude—be *gracious.*

Stay current, always up to date—be *relevant.*

As we begin to do this, Christianity becomes something that is absorbed, not just worn. It is more than believed; it is incarnated.

And if there is anything that will catch the attention of preoccupied people fighting the fires of the urgent, it is God's truth incarnated. It happened in the first century and it can happen in the twenty-first. Even in an aimless world like ours.

Strengthening Your Grip

Beautiful in God's Time

He has made everything beautiful in its time.

ECCLESIASTES 3:11, NKJV

🌿 Among Christians a favorite verse of Scripture is Romans 8:28: *And we know that God causes all things to work together for good to those who love God, to those who are called according to His purpose.*

The key part of the verse is "work together." That verse does not say "all things are good"—just as Solomon's comment does not say "everything is beautiful." It says, "All things are good as they work together for His purpose." This says, "He makes everything beautiful *in its time.*" And I've got news for those who struggle with God's timing. You may not live to see God's time completely fulfilled. You may live to a ripe old age, carry out your reason for existence, and die before the full program of God has reached its ultimate and completed purpose. But His promise stands—He will make everything beautiful in its time.

Living on the Ragged Edge

Wisdom Just in Time

*Do not worry about how or what
you are to say; for it will be given you
in that hour what you are to say.*

MATTHEW 10:19

Do you know what I've discovered about the Lord? He doesn't give wisdom on credit. He doesn't advance you a bundle of insight. . . . Do you know when He gives us words and wisdom and insight? *Right when we need them.* At the very instant they are required.

If you're a parent, you may have experienced this phenomenon. You find yourself in a situation you never anticipated, and couldn't prepare for. Suddenly, you're at one of the critical junctures of life where you're the mom or dad, and your child is looking into your eyes, depending on you for a right answer. Not always, but often, you are given the words you need. Later you realize that they were words beyond your own wisdom. At that quiet moment, you breathe a little prayer of thanks. "Praise You, Lord. That's exactly what needed to be said."

Moses: A Man of Selfless Dedication

The Sovereign Potter

But now, O LORD, You are our Father,
we are the clay, and You our potter; and
all of us are the work of Your hand.

By now in our Christian walk we hardly need the reminder that life is not a cloud-nine utopia. It is a terribly unrealistic view to think that Christ helps you live happily ever after; it's downright unbiblical! Most of life is learning and growing, falling and getting back up, forgiving and forgetting, accepting and going on.

We know the sovereign Potter is working with our clay as He pleases. I've watched a few potters at work. And it's a funny thing. I have seen them suddenly mash the clay down and start over again. Each time they do this, the clay comes out looking entirely different. And with gifted potters, they can start over and over—and each time it's better and better.

He is the Potter, we are the clay. He is the one who gives the commands; we are the ones who obey. . . . He is shaping us over into the image of His Son.

Day by Day with Charles Swindoll

WISDOM FOR THE WAY   131

God Made Me

> *You formed my inward parts;*
> *You wove me in my mother's womb.*
> *I will give thanks to You, for I am*
> *fearfully and wonderfully made.*
>
> PSALM 139:13–14

❧ The word *formed* literally means "originated or created." God reached into my life when I was merely a tiny embryo and began to shape me within. He originated me. He began to put me together while I was still in the soft silence of my mother's womb. It was there my "inward parts" were originated by God. . . .

The nine-month interweaving work of God included my likes and dislikes, my personality as well as my perspective on life. . . .

As I analyze my body and see the way I have been put together, I join the psalmist in praise and gratitude to God, my Creator. . . .

Mother Nature didn't make me. Fate did not shape me, neither was I just a biological combination of mother and dad in a moment of sexual passion. Nor was I conceived through blind chance. You, God (and no other), made me!

Growing Wise in Family Life

Leave It to God

> *The work of righteousness will be peace,*
> *and the service of righteousness,*
> *quietness and confidence forever.*
>
> ISAIAH 32:17

Can't seem to get where you want to go fast enough? *Leave it to God.*

Worried about your kids? *Leave it to God.*

Living in a place you'd rather not be? *Leave it to God.*

Looks like you won't graduate with honors? *Leave it to God.*

Found a lump and you see the doctor tomorrow? *Leave it to God.*

A mid-career change seems scary? *Leave it to God.*

You did the job but someone else got the credit? *Leave it to God.*

Day by Day with Charles Swindoll

Our Will or God's Will?

I will instruct you and teach you
in the way which you should go.

Following the will of God requires faith and action, which in turn call for risk and release. This is where things get very personal; this is where we persevere and flesh out the will of God.

I have come to this conclusion: Doing the will of God is rarely easy and uncomplicated. Instead, it is often difficult and convoluted. Or . . . *mysterious.* Because we don't know where He is taking us, we must bend our wills to His—and most of us are not all that excited about bending. We'd much prefer resisting. That's why Christian life is often such a struggle. I don't mean that it's a constant marathon of misery. It's just a struggle between our will and His will. Someday, when we are caught up with the Lord in glory, we will finally be all the things we have longed to be. Until then, we live in this never-ending tension of give and take, push and pull.

The Mystery of God's Will

Grace for Every
Shade of Sorrow

You have been distressed by various trials
so that the proof of your faith, . . . may be found
to result in praise and glory and honor. . . .

1 PETER 1:6–7

❧ Trials come in various forms. The word *various* comes from an interesting Greek term, *poikolos,* which means "variegated" or "many colored." We also get the term "polka dot" from it. Trials come in a variety of forms and colors. They are different, just as we are different. Something that would hardly affect you might knock the slats out from under me—and vice versa. But God offers special grace to match every shade of sorrow. . . .

This variety of trials is like different temperature settings on God's furnace. The settings are adjusted to burn off our dross, to temper us or soften us according to what meets our highest need. It is in God's refining fire that the authenticity of our faith is revealed. And the purpose of these fiery ordeals is that we may come forth as purified gold, a shining likeness of the Lord Jesus Christ Himself.

Hope Again

Take It by Faith

As the heavens are higher than the earth,
so are My ways higher than your ways,
and My thoughts than your thoughts.

ISAIAH 55:9

Despite all of our searching and all of our study of the Scriptures, we'll never be able to see everything clearly, to fully grasp and understand and answer all the questions. They are beyond our comprehension—a puzzle, a mystery.

In *Keep a Quiet Heart*, Elisabeth Elliott says, "Today is mine. Tomorrow is none of my business. If I peer anxiously into the fog of the future, I will strain my spiritual eyes so that I will not see clearly what is required of me now."

Much of what happens in life we simply have to take by faith. Answers will not be forthcoming. These are the tensions of reality, and if we get marooned on the tensions, we will not be able to travel further. That is as our heavenly Father planned it.

The Mystery of God's Will

A Dead-End Road

Pride goes before destruction, and
a haughty spirit before stumbling.

PROVERBS 16:17

🌺 What is it that drives us on so relentlessly? Are you ready? Take a deep breath and allow yourself to tolerate the one-word answer: PRIDE. We work and push and strive so we can prove we are worthy . . . we are the best . . . we deserve top honors. And the hidden message: I can gain righteousness all on my own, by my own effort, ingenuity, and energy. And because I can, I must! And why is this heretical? Because ultimately this philosophy says: (1) I really don't need divine righteousness (after all, God helps those who help themselves, right?), and (2) I will find lasting joy in my own achievement. This will bring me ultimate satisfaction.

Both are dead-end roads found on Fantasy Island.

Laugh Again

Great-Hearted Souls

Blessed are the peacemakers,
for they shall be called sons of God.

Peacemakers release tension, they don't intensify it. Peacemakers seek solutions and find no delight in arguments. Peacemakers calm the waters, they don't trouble them. Peacemakers work hard to keep an offense from occurring. And if it has occurred, they strive for resolution. Peacemakers lower their voices rather than raise them. Peacemakers generate more light than heat. Blessed are such great-hearted souls! . . .

Make no mistake, however; *peacemaker* is not a synonym for appeaser. This is not peace at any price. There are limits. . . . Smiling at wrongdoing or erroneous teaching doesn't simplify life; it complicates it.

When Christ blessed the peacemakers, He was extolling the value of doing all we can to maintain harmony and support unity. His interest was in making peace where peace is an appropriate objective.

Simple Faith

A Cluttered, Complicated World

> *God made us plain and simple,*
> *but we have made ourselves*
> *very complicated.*
>
> ECCLESIASTES 7:29, TEV

Everything around us works against reordering and simplifying our lives. Everything! Ours is a cluttered, complicated world. God did not create it that way. Depraved, restless humanity has made it that way!

Advertisements have one major goal: to make us discontented, woefully dissatisfied with who we are and what we have. Why? So we will acquire what they offer. And acquire we do! The watchword of our consumptive society is very loud and assertive—more! Enough is never enough. . . .

Not only do we acquire . . . we keep, we accumulate. Furthermore, we don't simply compete . . . we are driven to win, always win. And not only do we want more, we must spend more time maintaining those things. Staying ahead of that maddening pace leaves us strained, fretful, breathless.

Surely, God is not the author of such confusion.

Intimacy with the Almighty

Perfect in Him

He has now reconciled you . . .
in order to present you before [God]
holy and blameless and beyond reproach.

COLOSSIANS 1:22

Living as we do in a product-oriented culture, we like to package our faith, too. We prefer to sell a slick, shrink-wrapped version of salvation that includes happiness and peace, and happiness here and now, and heaven by and by. While there is nothing wrong with good marketing techniques or teaching principles of authentic success, there is something wrong if we neglect to mention the *process*, which must inevitably include times of defeat and failure. . . .

What I'd like to know is who erected such a happily-ever-after standard of perfection in the first place? God knows very well we aren't able to produce perfection; that's why Jesus, the perfect Son of God, placed us in His family. That's why He gave us a position of perfect righteousness in Him, reminding us by contrast that our own daily experience will constantly fall short.

Moses: A Man of Selfless Dedication

Root Out Rebellion

How blessed is the man who fears always,
but he who hardens his heart will fall into culamity.

❧ In a world hell-bent on having it's own way, it is terribly difficult to cultivate the right attitude toward authority. The "QUESTION AUTHORITY!" mentally is so interwoven into the fabric of our society, it seems impossible to counteract it. Realistically, about the only place we can come to terms with it is in our homes. Are you doing this? Be honest, now. Within the walls of your dwelling are you maintaining the controls? Maybe these three warnings will encourage you to stay at it . . . or start today.

Childhood. A rebellious nature is conceived in a home where parents relinquish control.

Adolescence. A rebellious spirit will be cultivated among peers who resist control. And if it isn't curbed there, it culminates at—

Adulthood. A rebellious life must be crushed by God when He regains control.

And take it from one who experienced it and deals with it week after week, nothing is more painful to endure.

Strengthening Your Grip

Wisdom

*When the wisdom of God
is at work in our life, we look at life
through lenses of perception, and we
respond to it in calm confidence.*

A Radical Decision

Keep sound wisdom and discretion. . . .
then you will walk in your way
securely, and your foot will not stumble.

PROVERBS 3: 21, 23

We are like tiny islands of truth surrounded by a sea of paganism, but we launch our ship every day. We can't live or do business in this world without rubbing shoulders with those driven by the world's desires. God calls very few to be monks in a monastery. So we must make a practical decision not to be conformed while are in the system, and at the same time, we must make a radical decision to give God the green light to transform our minds.

At the deepest level, even though the majority may not want to admit it, most people are conformists. That is why it is correctly termed a radical decision. Only a radically different mindset can equip folks like us to stand alone when we're outnumbered.

It takes courage to think alone, to resist alone, to stand alone—especially when the crowd seems so safe, so right.

Living Above the Level of Mediocrity

God's Gracious Liberty

*Our old self was crucified
with Him, in order that our body
of sin might be done away with.*

ROMANS 6:6

I remember one hot and humid Houston afternoon back in grade school when our teacher gave everyone permission to go barefoot after lunch. We got to pull off our socks, stick 'em in our sneakers, and wiggle our toes all we wanted to. During the afternoon recess that extra freedom added great speed to our softball game on the playground. . . .

Isn't it strange then, now that you and I are grown and have become Christians, how reluctant we are to give ourselves permission to do . . . to think . . . to say . . . to buy and enjoy . . . or to be different and not worry about who may say what?

Even though our God has graciously granted us permission to be free, to have liberty . . . and to enjoy so much of this life, many in His family seldom give themselves permission.

The Finishing Touch

Light and Truth

O send out Your light and Your truth,
let them lead me.

In this psalm David asks for two specific things: *light* and *truth*. He wanted God to give him His Word (truth) and an understanding of it (light). . . .

Every believer in Jesus Christ must ultimately come to the place where he is going to trust God's Word completely before he can experience consistent victory. It is our single source of tangible truth. We try every other crutch—we lean on self . . . on others . . . on feelings . . . on bank accounts . . . on good works . . . on logic and reason . . . on human perspective—and we continually end up with the short straw and churning. God has given His written Word and the promise of His light to all His children. When will we ever learn to believe it and live in it and use it and claim it? I often wonder how many of His personal promises to His people exist in His Book unclaimed and ignored.

Living Beyond the Daily Grind

God Takes Care of You

Be strong and courageous!
Do not tremble or be dismayed, for the LORD
your God is with you wherever you go.

JOSHUA 1:15

Did you know that worry erases the promises of God from your mind. Jesus implies this when He says, "O men of little faith. Do not be anxious then, saying, 'What shall we eat?' or 'With what shall we clothe ourselves?'" (Matthew 6:31) The promise of God is that He will not allow His children to beg bread. He will care for our needs and that's the promise you can claim. Since He took care of our greatest need at Calvary by giving us Christ, then you can be sure He will take care of everything else He considers important for us.

Perfect Trust

Triumphant Hope

The hope of the righteous is gladness.

One of the great themes of Christianity is triumphant hope. Not just hope as in a distant, vague dream, but *triumphant* hope, the kind of hope where all things end right. In the midst of the struggles and the storms and the sufferings of life, we can advance our thoughts beyond today and see relief . . . triumph . . . victory. Because, in the end, God does indeed win.

Think that through. All earthly woes, all financial pressures, all emotional trauma, all physical disabilities and handicaps, all domestic conflicts . . . all that ends. And we will be with Him who wins! And that means nothing but harmony and unity and victory and joy and praise and delight.

We'll be changed down inside. We'll have new natures. We'll have new minds. We'll have new bodies. We'll have the joy of living forever and ever in praise and adoration of our God.

Esther: A Woman of Strength and Dignity

Your Work Is Not in Vain

Let us not lose heart in doing good,
for in due time we will reap
if we do not grow weary.

Someone once counted all the promises in the Bible and came up with an amazing figure of almost 7500. Among that large number are some specific promises God's servants can claim today. Believe me, there are times when the only thing that will keep you going is a promise from God that your work is not in vain.

When we have done what was needed, but were ignored, misunderstood, or forgotten . . . we can be sure it was not in vain.

When we did what was right, with the right motive, but received no credit, no acknowledgement, nor even a "thank you" . . . we have God's promise that "we will reap."

The Finishing Touch

A Rare Commodity

A man's pride will bring him low,
but a humble spirit will obtain honor.

PROVERBS 29:23

Humility isn't a show we put on; in fact, if we think we're humble, we're probably not. And in our day of self-promotion, self-assertion, spotlighting "celebrities of the faith," and magnifying the flesh, this quality—so greatly valued by the Lord Jesus—is a rare commodity indeed. . . .

A truly humble person looks for opportunities to give himself freely to others rather than holding back, to release rather than hoarding, to build up rather than tearing down, to serve rather than being served, to learn from others rather than clamoring for the teaching stand. How blessed are those who learn this early in life.

Hope Again

Let Go, Relax

> *By wisdom a house is built,*
> *and by understanding it is established.*
>
> PROVERBS 24:3

The older I get the more I appreciate the benefits of taking time. Woodwork done slowly and meticulously by a craftsman is beautiful and able to endure the test of the elements. Art—whether musical compositions, needlework, sculpture, or painting—requires time and attention to detail. Even the cultivation of our walk with God . . . requires a great deal of time to develop.

The psalmist realized this when he wrote, "Be still, and know that I am God" (Psalm 46:10, NKJV). The Hebrew does not suggest standing around and letting your mind wander—not that kind of being still. Rather, it means "Let go, relax." . . .

If all this is true of other realms and responsibilities, it is certainly applicable to the home and family. Children were not created to be "jerked up" (as my mother used to put it), but to be cared for with gentleness and attention to detail. They require time . . . lots of it.

Growing Wise in Family Life

God Shows Himself Strong

Let your heart keep my commandments;
for length of days and years of life
and peace they will add to you.

PROVERBS 3:2

If you focus on the past, it won't be long before complaints start oozing from your lips. You will remember a long-ago time, bathed in a hazy, rosy glow of memory, when something was easier and more comfortable than it is today. And as you compare then and now, I guarantee it, you will grumble.

I do this; so do you. But it's so foolish! We look back nostalgically on what was once a pleasant situation, at which time (even then!) we were looking back longingly on a more pleasant earlier time. That's dumb, isn't it? You may be grumbling right now about your current situation. But chances are good that two years from now you'll be looking back on *this* moment and saying, "Oh for the good old days! Boy, it was great back then, wasn't it?" . . .

Stop! We live in the light of some dreamy past leisure or pleasure, when in actuality God continues to show Himself strong all along the way.

Moses: A Man of Selfless Dedication

In the Palm
of God's Hand

For the earth is the LORD'S, and all it contains.

1 CORINTHIANS 10:26

God has the whole world in His hands.
Remember the old gospel song? He's got the wind,
the rain, the tiny little baby, yes, even you and me
in His hands. How easy it is to forget that! And it
isn't limited to our geography or our culture, you
know. He's got the Middle East in His hands (that's
a relief, isn't it?), not to mention Central America
and Red China, Ethiopia and India, Indonesia and
Russia—all right there in the palms of His sovereign hands. And while we're at it, He's got our
future, our children, our circumstances, our
friends, and our foes in His hands . . . within His
grasp . . . under His control. Even when imaginary
fears slip in like the morning frost to blight our
faith, He's there—in charge. . . .

He has yesterdays' failures. He has today's challenges. He has tomorrow's surprises right there in
His hands. And not one of them causes Him to
gasp.

Living on the Ragged Edge

Everybody "Act Medium"

We love because He first loved us.

1 JOHN 4:19

The children worked long and hard on their little cardboard shack. It was to be a special spot—a clubhouse, where they could meet together, play, and have fun. Since a clubhouse has to have rules, they came up with three:

* Nobody act big.
* Nobody act small.
* Everybody act medium.

Not bad theology!

In different words, God says the very same thing: "Let each of you regard one another as more important than himself" (Phil. 2:3).

Just "act medium." Believable. Honest, human, thoughtful, and down-to-earth.

Day by Day with Charles Swindoll

Bless the Day of Rest

By the seventh day God completed His work which He had done, and He rested on the seventh day from all His work which He had done.

GENESIS 2:2

❧ Following the sixth day of creation, the Lord God deliberately stopped working. . . .

He rested. Take special note of that. It wasn't that there was nothing else He could have done. It certainly wasn't because He was exhausted—omnipotence never gets tired! He hadn't run out of ideas, for omniscience knows no mental limitations. He could easily have made many more worlds, created an infinite number of other forms of life, and provided multiple millions of galaxies beyond what He did.

But He didn't. He stopped.

He spent an entire day resting. In fact, He "blessed the seventh day and sanctified it," something He did not do on the other six days. He marked this one day off as extremely special. It was like no other. Sounds to me like He made the day on which He rested a "priority" period of time.

Strengthening Your Grip

Accept and Affirm
Each Other

*The wise in heart will be
called understanding, and sweetness
of speech increases persuasiveness.*

PROVERBS 16:21

🌿 God commands that we reach out, accept, and affirm one another. This means that we consciously resist the strong current of the stream we are in . . . the one that dictates all those excuses:

- "I'm just too busy."
- "It's not worth the risk."
- "I don't really need anyone."
- "If I reach out, I'll look foolish."

The devil's strategy for our times is working. He has deluded us into believing that we really shouldn't concern ourselves with being our brother's keeper. After all, we have time pressures and work demands (that relentless, fierce determination to be number one), not to mention, anxieties prompted by economic uncertainty. And who really needs our help anyway? I'll tell you who—just about every person we meet, that's who.

Strengthening Your Grip

The Whirlpool of Wickedness

His own iniquities will capture the wicked, and he will be held with the cords of his sin.

PROVERBS 5:22

❧ What a word picture! We usually think of this situation as applicable only to an unbeliever. But it could just as easily be applied to a Christian who deliberately chooses to disobey his Lord. And instead of seeing the error of his way, he stays in a state of carnality, which grieves the Spirit of God living within him. Carnality occurs when a believer deliberately operates in the strength of his or her own will . . . stubbornly refusing to acknowledge wrong and choosing to walk contrary to the teaching of Scripture. The promptings of God's Spirit are ignored as disobedience becomes a lifestyle. Choosing to live like that is like getting caught in a whirlpool. The wickedness intensifies. It gets more treacherous as he goes deeper into it. . . . Like the prodigal son, he winds up in misery and filth.

The Grace Awakening

Get Eternity
Securely in Place

He has also set eternity in
their heart, yet so that man will not
find out the work which God has done
from the beginning even to the end.

ECCLESIASTES 3:11

God has put eternity in our hearts. What in the
world does that mean? Well, let me help you with
the key word—*eternity.* Let's expand it to mean,
"curiosity about our future."

God has put within every human being's heart
a curiosity about tomorrow . . . an eternal capacity
that prompts me to probe, to be intrigued, to
search. That explains why your child—just about
the time that little fella or gal starts to run around
the house and talk—begins to ask questions about
tomorrow, about life, and about life beyond. . . . It's
the way God made human beings. God has not put
eternity in the heart of animals, only into the hearts
of men and women. And since that is true, since we
will not find out about tomorrow without God,
our pursuit must be of Him.

Living on the Ragged Edge

A Heart for the Task

For the eyes of the LORD move to and fro throughout the earth that He may strongly support those whose heart is completely His.

2 CHRONICLES 16:9

God's choices often seem so illogical from our point of view. We tell ourselves it can't be what He *really* means. . . .

Would you have singled out a sun-withered, eighty-year-old shepherd to face down one of the mightiest kings in the world? Moses had been out to pasture for forty years. He had completely lost touch with his people. He'd been raising a little family, living with and working for his father-in-law. In four decades the man couldn't scrape together enough shekels to build a little place of his own. Admit it, doesn't he seem like a highly unlikely prospect for the job of delivering an entire people group from the clutches of a mighty nation? . . .

God's eyes roam across the planet to find specific individuals whose hearts are just right for a particular task He has in mind. And when He finds them, watch out! He plunges them into the stream of action, upholding them with His mighty hand.

Moses: A Man of Selfless Dedication

Affection and Affirmation

The father of the righteous
will greatly rejoice, and he who sires
a wise son will be glad in him.

To you who bear the name "Dad," I cannot impress upon you enough how imperative it is that we show our affection. We can do that in two ways. First, we affirm who our child is; and second, we appreciate what our child does. This twofold assurance, however, must be given in more than words. Affection—the nonverbal communication of closeness—is among the most important experiences we share with our children. . . .

Unaffectionate dads, without ever wishing to do so, can trigger a daughter's promiscuity. All this leads me to write with a great deal of passion, dads . . . *don't hold back your affection!* Demonstrate your feelings of love and acceptance to both sons and daughters. . . . They will love you for it. And, more importantly, they will emulate your example when God gives them a family of their own.

Growing Wise in Family Life

Time Well-Spent

*Oil and perfume make the heart glad,
so a man's counsel is sweet to his friend.*

PROVERBS 27:9

❧ How valuable to *you* are relationships? If you have trouble answering that, I'll help you decide. Stop and think back over the past month or two. How much of your leisure time have you spent developing and enjoying relationships?

Jesus, God's Son, certainly considered the relationship He had with His disciples worth His time. They spent literally *hours* together. They ate together and wept together, and I'm sure they must have laughed together as well. Being God, He really didn't "need" those men. He certainly did not *need* the hassle they created on occasion. But He loved those twelve men. He believed in them. . . .

Whatever leisure time we are able to invest in relationships is time well spent. And when we do, let's keep in mind we are "imitating God," for His Son certainly did.

Strengthening Your Grip

Safe in God's Hands

I will not forget you!
See, I have engraved you
on the palms of my hands.

ISAIAH 49:16 NIV

❧ "The Lord has forsaken me . . . He has walked away . . . He has totally forgotten me." Ever said that? Of course you have! How about on Monday morning? You've just come off a glorious weekend retreat. Time in the Word. Great worship. . . . Lots of laughter. Meaningful prayer. . . . Then comes eight o'clock Monday morning back home, and your whole *world* caves in. "The Lord's forgotten me. He's completely left the scene."

But God says, "You are written on the palms of My hands. You are continually before me." . . .

Stop and glance at the palms of your hand. Now, imagine they are God's hands and that you are right there. . . . Our ways remain continually before Him. Not one fleeting moment of life goes by without His knowing exactly where we are, what we're doing, and how we're feeling.

Elijah: A Man of Heroism & Humility

The Benefits of Solitude

Every word of God is tested;
He is a shield to those who
take refuge in Him.

PROVERBS 30:5

The Scriptures are replete with references to the value of waiting before the Lord and spending time with Him. When we do, the debris we have gathered during the hurried, busy hours of our day gets filtered out, not unlike the silt that settles where a river widens. With the debris out of the way, we are able to see things more clearly and feel God's nudgings more sensitively.

David frequently underscored the benefits of solitude. I am certain he first became acquainted with this discipline as he kept his father's sheep. Later, during those tumultuous years when King Saul was borderline insane and pursuing him out of jealousy, David found his time with God not only a needed refuse but his means of survival. . . .

God still longs to speak to waiting hearts, . . . hearts that are quiet before Him.

The Finishing Touch

When God Says
It Will Be, It Will Be

I know you can do all things,
and that no purpose of Yours can be thwarted.

🌾 *"No purpose of Yours can be thwarted."* Remember that conclusion. . . . When God says it will be done, it will be done. If it makes me unhappy? It makes me unhappy. If it hurts? It hurts. If it ruins my reputation? It ruins my reputation. . . .

You want to know who's in charge around here? The One who called the spaces into being, the One who put the clouds in place, the One who established the atmosphere in which we're able to live, the One who separated the seas and the dry land, who gave you breath for your lungs and the ability to think. The One who placed you here, now in time, for His purpose, and the One who with the snap of His divine finger will pull you from life into eternity. Mysterious though our lives may seem, God, and God alone, is in charge.

The Mystery of God's Will

The Central Piece
of Life's Puzzle

My grace is sufficient for you,
for power is perfected in weakness.

2 CORINTHIANS 12:9

Suffering comes in many forms and degrees, but God's grace is always there to carry us beyond it. I've lived long enough and endured a sufficient number of trials to say without hesitation that only Christ's perspective can replace our resentment with rejoicing. Jesus is the central piece of suffering's puzzle. If we fit Him into place, the rest of the puzzle—no matter how complex and enigmatic—begins to make sense.

Only Christ's salvation can change us from spectators to participants in the unfolding drama of redemption. The scenes will be demanding. Some may be tragic. But only then will we understand the role that suffering plays in our lives. Only then will we be able to tap into hope beyond our suffering.

Hope Again

Count Your Blessings

Let us come before His presence
with thanksgiving. Let us shout joyfully
to Him with psalms.

PSALM 95:2

Sometimes when you don't feel like praying, or you're consumed with needing to speak to the Lord but can't gather the words, try that old standby— count your many blessings, count them one by one.

It's amazing how you can get carried away from worries and woes and self-concern when you start naming out loud what you're thankful for. Right away your focus shifts from your needs to the Father's graciousness and love.

Try it!

Day by Day with Charles Swindoll

Our Guide for Life

I will instruct you and teach you
in the way which you should go;
I will counsel you with My eyes upon you.

PSALM 32:8

When we arrive at dilemmas in life and are unable to decipher the right direction to go, if we hope to maintain our joy in the process, we must allow the Lord to be our Guide, our Strength, our Wisdom—our all! It's easy to read those words, but so tough to carry through on them. When we do, however, it's nothing short of remarkable how peaceful and happy we can remain. The pressure is on His shoulders, the responsibility is on Him, the ball is in His court, and an unexplainable joy envelops us . . .

To be sure, such an unusual method of dealing with dilemmas is rare—there aren't many folks willing to turn the reins over to God—and calls for humility, another rare trait among capable people. But it works! The Lord is a Master at taking our turmoil and revealing the best possible solution to us.

Laugh Again

The Power of Reconciliation

If you forgive others for their transgressions,
your heavenly Father will also forgive you.

MATTHEW 6:14

We cannot be right with God until we are right with one another.

The power of reconciliation is stronger than revenge. It is amazing how forgiveness unloads the weapon in the other person's hand. When you reconcile with your brother or sister, it is amazing what it does in both hearts. It is like having your nervous system flushed out. It is like getting over a longstanding fever and cleansing the corruption that has been diseasing your mind. You don't need an attorney for that. You probably don't need a minister or a counselor, either. You just need humility. To put it straight, in the final analysis you need guts. Don't wait any longer.

Keep it simple—go and make it right.

Simple Faith

Discover the Depths of God

Can you discover the limits of the Almighty?
They are high as the heavens, what can you do?

JOB 11:7–8

God's ways are not discovered through the normal, humanistic methods of research.

As important and intriguing as divine depths might be, they defy discovery by the natural means of our minds. God reserves these things for those whose hearts are completely His . . . for those who take the time to wait before Him. Only in that way can there be intimacy with the Almighty.

Tragically, precious little in this hurried and hassled age promotes such intimacy. We have become a body of people who look more like a herd of cattle in a stampede than a flock of God beside green pastures and still waters. Our forefathers knew, it seems, how to commune with the Almighty . . . but do we? We must learn anew to think deeply, to worship meaningfully, to meditate unhurriedly.

Intimacy with the Almighty

Let God Handle It

Cease striving and know that I am God.

PSALM 46:10

Sit down. That's right, my friend, *sit down!*

You have run far enough. You have stood long enough. You have fought, pushed, and manipulated your way for too many years. God has finally grabbed your attention. He is saying, "Quit! Stop! Let Me handle it! Sit there on the hot sands of the desert where you have brought yourself. Look at what lies next to you. It is a well, full of fresh water." Soon it will be God's delight to bring that bucket up and refresh your soul. Sit still. Stay there. Be quiet. . . .

Cease all the striving. Relax. Be contented by that well, and drink deeply. You are thirstier than you realize.

Moses: A Man of Selfless Dedication

True Excellence

No one can serve two masters.

MATTHEW 6:24

❧ If we hope to demonstrate the level of excellence modeled by Jesus Christ, then we'll have to come to terms with the kingdom we are going to serve: the eternal kingdom our Lord told us to seek (Matt. 6:33) or the temporal kingdom of today. . . .

Generally speaking, *God's kingdom is a synonym for God's rule.* Those who choose to live in His kingdom (though still very much alive on Planet Earth) choose to live under His authority.

For centuries God has been at work reestablishing His rulership. Jesus' words describe the problem: "No one can serve two masters; for either he will hate the one and love the other, or he will hold to the one and despise the other" (Matt. 6:24).

The kingdom is the invisible realm where God rules as supreme authority. . . . Only by letting Him reign in your life can you experience true excellence.

Living Above the Level of Mediocrity

Painted by God's Fingers

You visit the earth and
cause it to overflow, . . . You have
crowned the year with Your bounty.

PSALM 65:9, 11

Somewhere, miles away, crops push their way toward harvest and waves roar and tumble onto shore. Windswept forests sing their timeless songs, and desert animals scurry in the shadows of cactus and rock.

Within a matter of hours night will fall, the dark sky will glitter with moon and stars, and sleep will force itself upon us. Life will continue on uninterrupted. Appreciated or not, the canvas of nature will go on being painted by the fingers of God. . . .

In the midst of the offensive noise of our modern world—the people, the cars, the sounds, the smog, the heat, the pressures—there stand those reminders of His deep peace.

The Finishing Touch

Still, Small Nudges

Whom the LORD loves
He reproves, even as a father corrects
the son in whom he delights.

PROVERBS 3:12

What brings wisdom into our lives? Accepting God's reproofs. . . .

Reproof is from a Hebrew term that means "to correct . . . to convince." I often think of reproofs as God's proddings, those unmistakable nudges, His "still small voice." They are inner promptings designed to correct our ways. They alert us to the fact that we are off course. They communicate, in effect, "My child, that's wrong; change direction!"

These God-given reproofs sometimes appear in Scripture. . . . On other occasions the reproofs come verbally from those who love us. . . .

All of us have sagging character qualities that need attention. To ignore them is to open the gate that leads to disobedience.

Living Beyond the Daily Grind

Worry Is Worthless

My soul takes refuge in You;
and in the shadow of Your wings I will
take refuge until destruction passes by.

PSALM 57:1

Worry is a complete waste of energy. It solves nothing. That's why Jesus said, "Which of you by being anxious can add a single cubit to his life's span?" (Matt. 6:27) In essence He was saying, "You go to bed tonight and fret and fuss because you're not five feet, eleven inches; you're only five feet, nine inches. But when you wake up in the morning, you're still going to be five feet, nine inches." Worry will never make you stretch! And it won't solve that anxiety on your mind either.

Let me be completely candid here. Do you know why we worry? We have a quiet, hidden, *love* for worry. We enjoy it! When one worry is gone, we replace it with another. There's always a line of worries waiting to get in the door. So as one goes out the back door, we usher in the next one through the front door. We enjoy entertaining them. Worries are our mental and emotional companions. But Jesus says, in effect, that they're worthless!

Perfect Trust

Wisdom

*The more we glean God's wisdom,
the more strength we gain to live with
questions and tensions.*

An Attitude of Humility

Before destruction the heart of man is haughty,
but humility goes before honor.

PROVERBS 18:12

🌿 Humility is not how you dress, it is not the money you make, it is not where you live, it's not what you drive, it is not even how you look. We're never once commanded by God to "look" humble. Humility is an attitude. It is an attitude of the heart. An attitude of the mind. It is knowing your proper place. Never talking down or looking down because someone may be of a financial level less than yours. It is knowing your role and fulfilling it for God's glory and praise. I repeat, it is an attitude. . . .

The attitude Christ had, who emptied Himself of the voluntary and independent use of His divine attributes. There is no quality more god-like than humility. . . .

The place of highest exaltation, as we see in the Lord Jesus Christ, is a place of self-emptying humility. It's not a phony-baloney style of fake piety. It's true humility of mind. It's putting the other person first. . . . It is being like Christ.

Esther: A Woman of Strength and Dignity

Divine Relief

*It does not depend on the man
who wills or the man who runs,
but on God who has mercy.*

ROMANS 9:16

Few feelings bring a greater sense of satisfaction than relief, which Webster defines as "the removal or lightening of something oppressive, painful, or distressing." . . .

God calls this divine gift of relief mercy. That's right, *mercy*. It's a twin alongside *grace*. . . .

The essential link between God's grace and our peace is His mercy . . . that is, God's infinite compassion actively demonstrated toward the miserable. Not just pity. Not simply sorrow or an understanding of our plight, but divine relief that results in peace deep within.

The Finishing Touch

Brilliant Days, Broken Days

*I will strengthen you, surely I will
help you, surely I will uphold you
with My righteous right hand.*

ISAIAH 41:10

Our problem isn't that we've failed. Our problem is that we haven't failed enough. We haven't been brought low enough to learn what God wants us to learn. . . .

Remember one of the songs from the Seventies we used to sing again and again? It mentioned how we learned to trust in Jesus and to trust in God by going "through it all." Not around it. *Through* it.

Through it *all*. That's the ticket. Through the victories and the failures. . . . Through the brilliant days of accomplishment and the broken days. . . . Through the heady days of laughter and success and those nameless intervals of setback and blank despair. Through it all, He is with us, leading us, teaching us, humbling us, preparing us.

Moses: A Man of Selfless Dedication

Watch Those Choices!

Apply your heart to discipline
and your ears to words of knowledge.

PROVERBS 23:12

🌿 Living in truth is making the right choices. Here's what I mean. In the light of truth, you and I are able to see both truth and lie, both light and darkness—that which is simple, pure, and clear and that which is deceptive. . . .

The secret, of course, is making the right choices every day. So? Watch those choices! Watch your decisions!

No married couple suddenly splits. Nobody becomes a cynic overnight. Nobody makes one leap from the pinnacle of praise to the swamp of carnality. Erosion is a slow and silent process based on secret choices. And isn't it remarkable? If you don't stop yourself in the downward process, last week's wrong choice doesn't seem quite so bad this week. In fact, in a month's time it seems like not that bad a choice at all!

Simple Faith

Forget the Past

If anyone is in Christ,
he is a new creature,
the old things passed away;
behold, new things have come.

2 CORINTHIANS 5:17

🌿 Some of the unhappiest people I've ever known are living their lives looking over their shoulder. What a waste! Nothing back there can be changed.

What's in the past? Only two things: great attainments and accomplishments that could either make us proud by reliving them or indifferent by resting on them . . . or failures and defeats that cannot help but arouse feelings of guilt and shame. Why in the world would anyone want to return to that quagmire? I've never been able to figure that one out. By recalling those inglorious, ineffective events of yesterday, our energy is sapped for facing the demands of today. Rehearsing those wrongs, now forgiven in grace, derails and demoralizes us. There are few joy stealers more insidious than past memories that haunt our minds. . . . Forget the past!

Laugh Again

Managing Mistreatment

> *Sanctify Christ as Lord in your hearts,*
> *always being ready to make a defense to everyone*
> *who asks you to give an account for the hope that is*
> *in you, yet with gentleness and reverence.*

1 PETER 3:15

Anybody can accept a reward graciously, and many people can even take their punishment patiently when they have done something wrong. But how many people are equipped to handle mistreatment after they've done right? Only Christians are equipped to do that. . . .

When we think a wrong has been done to us that we don't deserve, we can respond, "Lord, You're with me right now. You are here, and You have Your reasons for what is happening. You will not take advantage of me. You're much too kind to be cruel. You're much too good to be unjust. You care for me too much to let his get out of hand. Take charge. Use my integrity to defend me. Give me the grace to stay calm. Control my emotions. Be Lord over my present situation. In such a prayer, we "sanctify Christ as Lord" in our hearts (1 Pet. 3:15).

Hope Again

A Cavalier Culture

There is a friend who
sticks closer than a brother.

PROVERBS 18:24

A hurry-up lifestyle results in a throwaway culture. Things that should be lasting and meaningful are sacrificed on the altar of the temporary and superficial.

The major fallout in such a setting is the habit of viewing relationships casually. This cavalier attitude cripples society in various ways:

Friends walk away instead of work through.

Partnerships dissolve rather than solve.

Neighbors no longer visit and relax together.

The aged are resented, not honored.

Husband and wives divorce rather than persevere.

Children are brushed aside rather than nourished.

Relationships! Never sell them short. If we'll slow down the hurry-up lifestyle for a moment and pause to catch our breath, we'll realize the need to call a halt to our throwaway culture.

Growing Wise in Family Life

Let Go and Let God

> *Do not fear! Stand by and*
> *see the salvation of the LORD which*
> *He will accomplish for you. . . .*
>
> EXODUS 14:13

We Americans use a number of words to describe a predicament. If you're from the East, you probably know about "being in a pinch." If you like to cook, you're "in a jam," or "in a pickle." If you're from the South, you're "between a rock and a hard place." . . . It may be that right now you find yourself in a predicament. . . .

And what should your response be?

Most people are prone to say, "God helps those who help themselves." People think that despicable saying comes from the Bible, but it doesn't. It's from the pit. No, God helps *the helpless!* As long as we're helping ourselves, who needs God? It's when we reach the end of our tether, and we're dangling out in space, that we finally cry out, "God, help me!" And God says, "I will. *Let go.*"

Letting go works against human nature. But God wants us to do just that—to freefall into His everlasting arms and trust completely in Him.

Moses: A Man of Selfless Dedication

The End of the Story

The end of a matter is better than its beginning. . . .
Wisdom along with an inheritance is good. . . .
For wisdom is protection just as money is protection.

ECCLESIASTES 7:8, 11, 12

❀ *"The end of a matter is better than its beginning."* That makes sense doesn't it? You see, the end of a matter is maximum reality. Those little idealistic dreams have ended. The whole truth is on display. . . . The complete picture has developed. Once we reach the end, we know the whole story, and that is better than the beginning of a matter where desires lack substance.

I had a grandfather tell me recently that he plans to put a lot of his thoughts on a cassette tape because, he said, "I don't know how long I'm gonna live and I don't know how long I'll have my mind, so I'm gonna record some important counsel and let my grandchildren listen to it later on."

The most influential man in my life was my mother's father. I can still hear his wise counsel. Such counsel is better than most advice given to a child because it is end-of-the-matter information coming from one who has been seasoned with wisdom.

Living on the Ragged Edge

Leisure Is Free

> *A little sleep, a little slumber;*
> *a little folding of the hands to rest.*
>
> PROVERBS 24:33

❧ Please understand that leisure is more than idle free time not devoted to paid occupations. Some of the most valuable work done in the world has been done at leisure . . . and never paid for in cash. Leisure is free activity. Labor is compulsory activity. In leisure, we do what we like, but in labor we do what we must. In our labor we meet the objective needs and demands of others—our employer, the public, people who are impacted by and through our work. But in leisure we scratch the subjective itches within ourselves. In leisure our minds are liberated from the immediate, the necessary. As we incorporate leisure into the mainstream of our world, we gain perspective. We lift ourselves above the grit and grind of mere existence.

Interestingly, leisure comes from the Latin word *licere*, which means "to be permitted." If we are ever going to inculcate leisure into our otherwise utilitarian routine, we must give ourselves permission to do so.

Strengthening Your Grip

Aligned to God's Will

The fruit of the righteous is a tree of life,
and he who is wise wins souls.

PROVERBS 11:30

If we were asked to respond with yes or no to the question, all of us would say, "Yes, I want to know [God's] will." But *doing* God's will is another matter entirely, because almost without exception it requires risk and adjustment and change. We don't like that. Even using those words makes us squirm. Experiencing the reality of them is even worse. We love the familiar. We love the comfortable. We love something we can control—something we can get our arms around. Yet the closer we walk with the Lord, the less control we have over our own lives, and the more we must abandon to Him. To give Him our wills and to align our wills to His will requires the abandonment of what we prefer, what we want or what we would choose.

The Mystery of God's Will

A Rat in the Corner of Life

Are not two sparrows sold for a cent?
And yet not one of them will fall to
the ground apart from your Father.

MATTHEW 10:29

Maybe you have a worry related to some simple, daily problem that eats away at your peace, like a rat in the corner of your life. It just gnaws and gnaws and gnaws. You can't seem to get out from under it. Maybe it was a foolish mistake you made and you're paying for it. . . .

[One] problem with worry is that *it makes you forget your worth*. Worry makes you feel worthless, forgotten, and unimportant. That's why Jesus says that we are worth much more than the birds of the air who neither worry nor die of hunger because their heavenly Father feeds them (Matthew 6:26). They enjoy what's there. If God is able to sustain the lesser creatures, won't He sustain the greater? Maybe you're worried about things that seem important in your life. Yet your heavenly Father knows what is essential better than you do. And you are worth so much that He is taking things one at a time, dealing with more important things right now in your life.

Perfect Trust

Deflating Pride

Look to the rock from which you were hewn,
and to the quarry from which you were dug.

ISAIAH 51: 1

In the Hebrew text, the word *quarry* actually refers to "a hole." The old King James Version doesn't miss it far: "the hole of the pit whence ye are digged." Never forget "the hole of the pit."

What excellent advice! Before we get all enamored with our high-and-mighty importance, it's a good idea to take a backward glance at the "hole of the pit" from which Christ lifted us. And let's not just *think* about it; let's admit it. Our "hole of the pit" has a way of keeping us all on the same level— recipients of grace. And don't kid yourself, even those who are extolled and admired have "holes" from which they were dug.

- With Moses, it was murder.
- With Peter, it was public denial.
- With Rahab, it was prostitution.

The next time we're tempted to become puffed up by our own importance, let's just look back to the pit from which we were dug. It has a way of deflating our pride.

Strengthening Your Grip

The Soul Belongs to God

And my soul shall rejoice in the LORD;
it shall exult in His salvation.

PSALM 35:9

Nothing physical touches the soul. Nothing external satisfies our deepest inner needs. Remember that! The soul belongs to God. He alone can satisfy us in that realm.

The soul possesses an inescapable God-shaped vacuum. And not until He invades and fills it can we be at peace within—which is another way of saying, "If God isn't in first place, you can't handle success." If God fills your soul, if God fills your mind, if God satisfies your spirit, there is no problem whatsoever with prosperity. You've got it all put together. Your priorities will be right, and you will know how to handle you life so you can impact the maximum number of people. If He prospers you, if He entrusts you with material success and you continue walking with Him, God can use you mightily in His plan. Furthermore, if you lose it all, He can give you what it takes to handle the loss and start all over again.

Living on the Ragged Edge

We Want Relief

> *I love the LORD, because He hears my voice and my supplications. Because He has inclined His ear to me, therefore shall I call upon Him as long as I live.*
>
> <small>PSALM 116:1–2</small>

🌿 Do you ever find yourself saying something like this? "Lord, I give You my life, but I'm weary to death of this irritation, this person, this circumstance, this uncomfortable situation. I feel trapped, Lord. I want relief—I must have relief! And if You don't bring it soon . . . well, I've had it. I feel like walking away from it all."

You may walk, my friend, but there are no shortcuts. Here's a better plan: Reach for the hand of your Guide! He is Lord of the desert. Even your desert. The most precious object of God's love is His child in the desert. If it were possible, you mean more to Him during this time than at any other time. . . . You are His beloved student taking his toughest courses. He loves you with an infinite amount of love.

Moses: A Man of Selfless Dedication

A Dad's Greatest Gift

Hear, O sons, the instruction of a father, and give attention that you may gain understanding.

PROVERBS 4:1

Dad, is it possible you've gotten overly committed, so involved in your work or some away-from-home project or hobby that it is draining your time and energy with your family? I understand, believe me, I do. . . .

Instead of challenging fathers to give of themselves, our cultural system encourages them to give the stuff their increased salaries can buy—a better education, a membership at the club, material possessions, nicer homes, extra cars. . . . But what about dad himself? And that priceless apprenticeship learned in his presence? . . . It's gotten lost in the shuffle. . . .

C'mon, dads, let's lead a revolt! Let's refuse to take our cues from the system any longer. Let's start saying no to more and more of the things that pull us farther and farther away from the ones who need us the most. Let's remember that the greatest earthly gifts we can provide are our presence and influence while we live and a magnificent memory of our lives once we're gone.

Growing Wise in Family Life

Face to Face with God

God will bring every act to judgment,
everything which is hidden,
whether it is good or evil.

ECCLESIASTES 12:4

If God says that He will bring every act to judgment, . . . I know He will. I don't know His method and frankly, that doesn't bother me. What ought to bother us is that He will do it! . . . Somehow in God's own timing and in God's own way, He will cause there to be a replay of our lives. . . . It makes a lot of sense to me that the One who made us has every right to hold us accountable. . . .

We cannot live the life of an irresponsible playboy and get away with it. We aren't free to run wild and wink in God's direction, thinking that, no matter what, the big Teddy Bear in the sky will yawn, pat us on the head, and say, "Everything is going to be just fine." No, it doesn't work like that. Our ragged-edge journey is headed for a sudden stop. And all alone, standing face to face with God in that epochal moment, we will give an account of the life we have lived.

Sober, serious thought!

Living on the Ragged Edge

Hold onto God's Hand

Seek the LORD and His strength;
seek His face continually

PSALM 105:4

❧ Discovering and embracing God's will leads us to make major adjustments. And that requires us to release and risk—releasing the familiar and risking whatever the future may bring. That's the bottom line of fleshing out God's will. . . .

We are only finite human beings. We can only see the present and the past. The future is a little frightening to us. So we need to hold onto God's hand and trust Him to calm our fears. And at those times when we're stubborn and resisting and God shakes us by the shoulders to get our attention, we're reminded that we don't call our own shots, that God has a plan for us, mysterious though it may seem, and we want to be in the center of it.

All the risks notwithstanding, that's still the safest place on earth to be.

The Mystery of God's Will

Sensitive Rather than Strong

Husbands, love your wives,
just as Christ also loved the church
and gave Himself up for her.

EPHESIANS 5:25

God's goal for us as husbands is to be sensitive rather than to prove how strong and macho we are. We need to love our wives, listen to them, adapt to their needs. We need to say no to more and more in our work so we can say yes to more and more in our homes . . . so we can say yes to the needs of our children and our families. (How else will your children learn what it means to be a good husband and father?)

Mind you, this is not to be a smothering kind of attention—the kind that says a husband is so insecure he cannot let his wife out of his sight. Instead, this is the kind of love that means your wife can't come back fast enough to your arms.

Hope Again

God's Mysterious Plan

I am the LORD, and there is no other;
besides Me there is no god.

ISAIAH 45:5

❀ There are occasions when we are surprised by God's decreed will . . . like when we get the results back from our physical exam and the MRI reveals a tumor we had no idea was there. . . . Or when the stock market plunges in one day to a ten-year, record-setting low.

It may seem to many that the One who made us is too far removed to concern Himself with such tiny details of life on this old globe. But that is not the case. His mysterious plan is running its course right on schedule, exactly as He decreed it.

This world is not out of control, spinning wildly through space. Nor are earth's inhabitants at the mercy of some blind, random fate. When God created the world and set the stars in space, He also established the course of this world and His plan for humanity.

The Mystery of God's Will

The Heartbeat of the Home

Cease listening, my son, to discipline,
and you will stray from the words of knowledge.

PROVERBS 19:27

The birth of a child is not taken lightly by the Lord. Each one is significant. Each one is viewed by God as a transfer of love from His heart to the couple receiving the gift.

God never wastes parents. He doesn't inadvertently "dump" kids haphazardly into homes. Nor does He deliver "accidents" into our lives. It is exceedingly important that families place the same significance on children that God does. Again, this is contrary to the mentality of many people in our society today. We are considered as somewhere between weird and ignorant if we have this kind of attitude toward children, especially if we have a large number of them. . . .

It is axiomatic. Healthy, well-disciplined, loving homes produce people who make a nation peaceful and strong. As the family goes, so goes the nation. When you boil it down to the basics, the pulse of an entire civilization is determined by the heartbeat of its homes.

Strengthening Your Grip

Humble in Heart

Take my yoke and learn from Me,
for I am gentle and humble in heart,
and you will find rest for your souls.

MATTHEW 11:29

What is the most Christ-like attitude on earth?
Think before you answer too quickly. I am certain
many would answer *love*. That is understandable,
for He did indeed love to the uttermost. Others
might say *patience*. Again, not a bad choice. I find
no evidence of impatience or anxious irritability as
I study His life. *Grace* would also be a possibility.
No man or woman ever modeled or exhibited the
grace that He demonstrated right up to the
moment He breathed His last.

As important as those traits may be, however,
they are not the ones Jesus Himself referred to
when He described Himself for the only time in
Scripture. . . . "I am gentle and humble in heart . . ."
(Matt. 11:29), . . . which might best be summed up
in the one word *unselfish*. According to Jesus' testimony, that is the most Christ-like attitude we can
demonstrate.

Laugh Again

A Message
for the Marketplace

Whatever your hand finds to do,
do it with all your might.

ECCLESIASTES 9:10

❧ I'm just maverick enough to say that I think fewer Christian ought to be going into the ministry and more should be going into business and into occupations that have nothing to do with the vocational Christian service. I don't see life divided into public and private, secular and sacred. It's all an open place of service before our God. My hope is to see . . . a group of Christians who will infiltrate our society—in fact, our entire world—with a pure, beautiful message of grace and honesty in the marketplace.

Recently I had a delightful talk with a keen-thinking young man . . . at our church. As we visited, I asked him about his future plans. "Well, I've just graduated from law school," he said. When I asked about how he hoped to use his training, he said, "I want to be a man of integrity who practices law." What refreshing words! They reflected the right priority.

Simple Faith

Faith for the Future

*[I rejoice] to see your good discipline
and the stability of your faith in Christ.*

COLOSSIANS 2:5

The nature of the beast within all of us resists change. Even though our past has been painful and in some ways unrewarding and perhaps even unproductive, it would be interesting to know how many of us would rather return to our past than face the uncertainty of our future. Being creatures of habit, we would rather have the security of our yesterday than the uncertainty of our tomorrow.

But it's the uncertainty of our future that really strengthens our faith. I mean, if we knew what it was all about, then it would take no faith. All it would take is obedience. If you knew what was going to happen in the next ten years of your life, what kind of faith would it take to walk that path?

It's the mystery of it all that gives it the power, the mystery of the whole process called God's working that makes the power so magnificent.

Dropping Your Guard

Your Fingerprints or God's?

The way of the LORD is
a stronghold to the upright,
but ruin to the workers of iniquity.

PROVERBS 10:29

❧ You cannot sow a fleshly seed and reap a spiritual plant. You cannot plant a carnal act and grow spiritual fruit. If you manipulate and connive and scheme and lie to get yourself to the top, don't thank God for the promotion! God knows, as you know, that you maneuvered and pulled strings. . . . So when you get that bigger office and the key to the executive washroom, don't give Him the credit. He doesn't want it. Your fingerprints are all over that scheme, not His.

At times we say to the Lord, "Thanks for that, Father." And the Lord must answer back, "Who? Me? I didn't pull that off. That was *your* doing." . . . You fudge on your income tax, get a nice refund and thank Him for the extra cash you can give to the building fund.

It doesn't work that way, friend. He says to you, "This isn't My doing. This is your plan."

Moses: A Man of Selfless Dedication

A Joyful Heart

> *You have put gladness in my heart.*
>
> PSALM 4:7

❧ We need to lighten up! Yes, spirituality and fun do go well together. Scripture speaks directly to this issue, you know: "A joyful heart makes a cheerful face, but when the heart is sad the spirit is broken" (Prov. 15:13). . . .

We're not talking about a person's face here as much as we are about the heart. Internal joy goes public. We can't hide it. The face takes its cue from an inside signal.

A well-developed sense of humor reveals a well-balanced personality. . . . The ability to get a laugh out of everyday situations is a safety valve. It rids us of tensions and worries that could otherwise damage our health.

You think I'm exaggerating the benefits? If so maybe you've forgotten another proverb: "A joyful heart is good medicine . . ." (Prov. 17:22). What is it that brings healing to the emotions, healing to the soul? A joyful heart!

Living Above the Level of Mediocrity

God's Will and Ways

> *As the deer pants for*
> *the water brooks, so my soul*
> *pants for You, O God.*
>
> PSALM 42:1

Godliness is something below the surface of a life, deep down in the realm of attitude—an attitude toward God Himself.

The longer I think about this, the more I believe that a person who is godly is one whose heart is sensitive toward God, one who takes God seriously. . . . . The godly individual hungers and thirsts after God. In the words of the psalmist, the godly person has a soul that "pants" for the living God (Ps. 42:1–2).

Godly people possess an attitude of willing submission to God's will and ways. Whatever He says goes. And whatever it takes to carry it out is the very thing the godly desire to do.

The Finishing Touch

Our Weakness, His Strength

*Wait for the LORD; be strong
and let your heart take courage;
yes, wait for the LORD.*

PSALM 27:14

Let's look at that term *wait*. It is from the Hebrew verb *kah-wah* meaning "to twist, stretch." The noun form means "line, cord, thread." A vivid picture emerges here. It is a verb describing the making of a strong, powerful rope or cord by twisting and weaving ourselves so tightly around the Lord that our weaknesses and frail characteristics are replaced by His power and unparalleled strength. It describes very literally the truth of what has been termed the "exchanged life." As we wait on God, our weakness is exchanged for His strength.

Strength and courage are developed *during* a trial, not after it is over.

Living Beyond the Daily Grind

Walking with God

It is better to take refuge in
the LORD than to trust in a man.

PSALM 118:8

Walking with God is the most exciting and rewarding of all experiences on earth. I should add, it is also the most difficult. I don't think I've ever met an exception to the rule, that those who walk closest to God are those who, like Jesus, become acquainted with trials and testings. God takes us through struggles and difficulties so that we might become increasingly more committed to Him. . . .

God may be leading you somewhere . . . that doesn't make much sense. I want to encourage you: Don't try to make sense out of it, just go. If God leads you to stay in a difficult situation and you have peace that you are to stay, don't analyze it, stay. Do your part. Do what He tells you to do, for His promises often hinge on obedience. . . .

You can walk with Him in perfect trust. That's your part.

Perfect Trust

Self-Control Is Inner Strength

The fruit of the Spirit is love, joy, peace, patience, kindness, goodness, faithfulness, gentleness, self-control.

Every one of us has gotten angry and lost our tempers, only to regret it. Every one of us has allowed our schedules to get so overloaded that, looking back over the week, we must admit to ourselves, if we're honest, we've not stopped to pray even once. Every one of us has eaten too much, even when we swore we wouldn't. Who hasn't fought yet again the old battle with lust or greed or materialism or anger or envy? . . .

There is an answer to this daily dilemma, a solution that is easy to identify. There is a secret to holding back. . . .

"Self-control" . . . that's the key . . . that's the answer. . . .

The best synonym for self-control is "discipline." . . . Self-control means "inner strength."

The fruit of the Spirit is self-control. Self-control frees us from slavery. Self-control stops bad habits. It checks us. It halts us.

Esther: A Woman of Strength and Dignity

Wisdom

*Wisdom is the God-given ability
to see life with rare objectivity
and to handle life with rare stability.*

Diligence and Faithfulness

Serve the LORD with gladness:
come before him with joyful singing.

PSALM 100:2

Servanthood implies diligence, faithfulness, loyalty, and humility.

Servants don't compete . . . or grandstand . . . or polish their image . . . or grab the limelight. They know their job, they admit their limitations, they do what they do quietly and consistently.

Servants cannot control anyone or everything, and they shouldn't try.

Servants cannot change or "fix" people. . . .

Servants cannot concern themselves with who gets the credit. . . .

Let's serve . . . in the name of Jesus.

The Finishing Touch

Only Character Endures

I have walked in my integrity
and I have trusted in the LORD
without wavering.

PSALM 26:1

Nothing speaks louder or more powerfully than a life of integrity. Absolutely nothing! Nothing stands the test like solid character. You can handle the blast like a steer in a blizzard. The ice may form on your horns, but you keep standing against the wind and the howling, raging storm because Christ is at work in your spirit. Character will always win the day. As Horace Greeley wrote: "Fame is a vapor, popularity an accident, riches take wing, and only character endures."

There is no more eloquent and effective defense than a life lived continually and consistently in integrity. It possesses invincible power to silence your slanderers.

Hope Again

Hurried, Harried Homes?

Know well the condition of your flocks,
and pay attention to your herds.

PROVERBS 27:23

🌿 What's the atmosphere like in your home these days? . . . Are you in danger of raising a "hurried child?" Capture some time this week and take an honest look at the quality of childhood your family lifestyle is providing for your little ones. What will be memorable to your kids when they, as adults, look back on the early years? Will it all seem like a high-pressure blur to them . . . one long breathless marathon? Have you allowed television to snatch up much of your children's unscheduled minutes . . . and *hours?*

Seeking God's wisdom, ask yourselves, "What can we do as mom and dad to encourage our kids to enjoy being *kids.*" Are you creating an atmosphere of relaxation and flexibility . . . or do the words *hurry* and *rigidity* better characterize your home? Any plans for a relaxed family vacation in the works? . . . As you plan, remember that childhood is an infinitely precious commodity. Your children will only grow up once.

Growing Wise in Family Life

The Beauty
of God's Holiness

Holy, holy, holy is the Lord God,
the Almighty, who was and who is
and who is to come.

REVELATION 4:8

We live in a day of pitifully shallow concepts of God. Some of today's contemporary Christian music leaves the impression that God is our buddy—a great pal to have in a pinch. . . . One pop song asks, "What if God were just a slob like us?" That is not the biblical view of God. That is man's feeble attempt to make God *relevant*.

Do you hear the cheap twang of such a concept of God? These small ideas of Him diminish the beauty of His holiness. . . .

The Puritans, that rigorous people of old, possessed a solidly biblical concept of God. Do you know why it is so crucial for us to recover such a respectful understanding? Because a shallow view of God leads to a shallow life. Cheapen God and you cheapen life itself. Treat God superficially, and you become superficial.

Moses: A Man of Selfless Dedication

Undeserved Kindness

> *But we believe that we are saved*
> *through the grace of the Lord Jesus.*
>
> ACTS 15:11

If you have traveled to London, you have perhaps seen royalty. If so, you may have noticed sophistication, aloofness, distance. On occasion, royalty in England will make the news because someone in the ranks of nobility will stop, kneel down, and touch or bless a commoner. That is grace. There is nothing in the commoner that deserves being noticed or touched or blessed by the royal family. But because of grace in the heart of the queen, there is the desire at that moment to pause, to stoop, to touch, even to bless. . . .

To show grace is to extend favor or kindness to one who doesn't deserve it and can never earn it. Receiving God's acceptance by grace always stands in sharp contrast to earning it on the basis of works. Every time the thought of grace appears, there is the idea of its being undeserved. In no way is the recipient getting what he or she deserves. Favor is being extended simply out of the goodness of the heart of the giver.

The Grace Awakening

Stop the Blame Game

He who conceals his transgressions
will not prosper, but he who confesses
and forsakes them will find compassion.

PROVERBS 28:13

Let's not kid ourselves. When we deliberately choose not to stay positive and deny joy a place in our lives, we'll usually gravitate in one of two directions, sometimes both—the direction of blame or self-pity. . . .

The aggressive attitude reacts to circumstances with blame. We blame ourselves or someone else, or God, or if we can't find a tangible scapegoat, we blame "fate." What an absolute waste! When we blame ourselves, we multiply our guilt, we rivet ourselves to the past (another "dangling" unchangeable), and we decrease our already low self-esteem. If we choose to blame God, we cut off our single source of power. Doubt replaces trust, and we put down roots of bitterness that can make us cynical. If we blame others, we enlarge the distance between us and them. . . .We settle for something much less than God ever intended. And on top of all that, we do not find relief!

Strengthening Your Grip

Welcome Wise Rebukes

Better is open rebuke
than love that is concealed.

PROVERBS 27:5

❧ Hearing a wise person's rebuke is far better than humming a fool's song. That's the idea. Most of us fail to hear the rebukes of the wise. Sometimes the wise person is a boss who attempts to evaluate our job. At other times it's a parent who pulls us up close, in one of those nose-to-nose encounters, and tells us some things we need to hear. But we find such occasions difficult to bear. . . .

Are we listening to the rebuke of the wise? Sometimes the wise rebuke comes from a former mate. Or the wise person could be a pastor, or a therapist, or a physician, or an attorney. We must be open and willing to learn from rebukes.

Living on the Ragged Edge

Stubborn Sometimes

> *Do not be as the horse or as the mule*
> *which have no understanding. . . .*
>
> PSALM 32:9

You've heard of God's children referred to as sheep. It isn't a bad picture, all things considered. The image conjures up visions of green pastures, still waters, and a gentle Shepherd, keeping watch over the flock.

But He also refers to us as mules. Sometimes, I think that's a better analogy.

Don't be like a balky mule! Don't be stubborn when God speaks. Don't continually fight and resist Him. Don't keep running away from Him so that He can't speak to you. Don't force Him to lasso you before you'll let Him draw near.

Why do we resist such a magnificent God who loves us? It makes no sense!

Moses: A Man of Selfless Dedication

Developing Secure Children

A man who loves wisdom makes his father glad.

PROVERBS 29:3

If parents were to ask me, "What is the greatest gift we could give our young child?" I would answer rather quickly: a sensitive spirit. That is especially rare among busy parents who live under the demands of hurried schedules, constantly doing battle with the tyranny of the urgent. Nevertheless, my counsel to you would be, give your child the time it takes to find out how he or she is put together. Help you child know who he or she is. Discuss those things with your children. Help them know themselves so that they learn to love and accept themselves as they are. Then, as they move into a society that seems committed to pounding them into another shape, they will remain true to themselves, secure in their independent walk with God.

I have begun to realize that secure, mature people are best described in fifteen words. They know who they are . . . they like who they are . . . they are who they are. They are *real*.

Growing Wise in Family Life

The Fairest Flower

> *O LORD, my heart is not proud,*
> *nor my eyes haughty; nor do I involve*
> *myself in great matters.*
>
> PSALM 131:1

Genuine humility isn't something we can announce very easily. To claim this virtue is, as a rule, to forfeit it. Humility is the fairest and rarest flower that blooms. Put it on display and instantly it wilts and loses its fragrance! . . . No, humility is not something to be announced. It simply belongs in one's life, in the private journal of one's walk with God.

There are two simple and quick ways God says the true condition of the heart is revealed. The first is through the eyes and the second is through the mouth (Luke 6:45). . . . Keen counselors and wise people are careful to listen to words (what is said as well as what *isn't* said) and watch the eyes of others. You soon discover that the heart is like a well and the eyes and tongue are like buckets that draw water from the same well. If true humility is not in the heart, the eyes will show it.

Living Beyond the Daily Grind II

God Is All in All

The king's heart is like channels of water in the hand of the LORD; He turns it wherever He wishes.

God rules, God reigns. God, and God alone. And His way is right. It leads to His glory.

Deep within the hearts of men and women, even though most would never acknowledge it, is the realization that we really don't have the final answer. There is this little hidden clause tucked away in the deep recesses of most thinking minds that says, "There may be a God after all."

When we take this to the ultimate future for humanity, God is sovereignly in charge. One second after they die, the men and women who have rejected and resisted the Lord for years will step into eternity. One second . . . and they will be totally at a loss to determine their future. God's sovereignty steps over their lives and sets forth His decree, "That God may be all in all."

The Mystery of God's Will

Let God Build Your House

Unless the LORD builds the house,
they labor in vain who build it.

PSALM 127:1

🌿 Here's the idea. During those all-important early months and years of marriage, make sure that the Lord your God is the heart and center of your family! If He is not, the whole experience is a study in futility—a wasted, empty, counterproductive effort. It will all be in vain. He doesn't have in mind a home that hangs a lot of religious mottos on the walls or a couple that simply goes to church regularly or offers up a quick prayer before meals or places a big Bible on the living room coffee table. No, the essential ingredient is "the Lord."

A family gets started on the right foot when Jesus Christ is in each life (husband and wife are both born again), and when the lengthening shadow of His Lordship pervades that relationship. When a couple makes Christ a vital part of their life, in the terms of the psalm, that's when "the Lord builds the house."

Strengthening Your Grip

Nothing Helps Like Hope

Let us hold fast the confession
of our hope without wavering,
for He who promised is faithful.

HEBREWS 10:23

Hope is a wonderful gift from God, a source of strength and courage in the face of life's harshest trials.

When we are trapped in a tunnel of misery, hope points to the light at the end.

When we are overworked and exhausted, hope gives us fresh energy.

When we are discouraged, hope lifts our spirits.

When we are tempted to quit, hope keeps us going.

When we struggle with a crippling disease or a lingering illness, hope helps us persevere beyond the pain.

When we fear the worst, hope brings reminders that God is still in control.

When we are forced to sit back and wait, hope gives us the patience to trust.

Put simply, when life hurts and dreams fade, nothing helps like hope.

Hope Again

The Pursuit of Happiness

For to me, to live is Christ,
and to die is gain.

PHILIPPIANS 1:21

When money is our objective, we must live in fear of losing it, which makes us paranoid and suspicious.

When fame is our aim, we become competitive lest others upstage us, which makes us envious.

When power and influence drive us, we become self-serving and strong-willed, which makes us arrogant.

And when possessions become our god, we become materialistic, thinking enough is never enough, which makes us greedy.

All these pursuits fly in the face of contentment . . . and joy.

Only Christ can satisfy, whether we have or don't have, whether we are known or unknown, whether we live or die. . . . The pursuit of happiness is the cultivation of a Christ-centered, Christ-controlled life.

Laugh Again

Hand-in-Hand

*Make my joy complete by being of
the same mind, maintaining the same love,
united in spirit, intent on one purpose.*

PHILIPPIANS 2:1

It is only when I *share* life's experiences with others that I can enjoy them or endure them to the greatest advantage. This is what the early Christians did. They learned quickly that survival would go hand-in-hand with "fellowship." . . .

You see, having a relationship calls for being in fellowship with others, and that cannot be done very easily at arm's length. It implies getting in touch, feeling the hurts, being an instrument of encouragement and healing. Fences must come down. Masks need to come off. Welcome signs need to be hung outside the door. Keys to the locks in our lives must be duplicated and distributed. Bridges need to be lowered that allow others to cross the moat and then share our joys and our sorrows.

Dropping Your Guard

The Blessed Life

Blessed are the pure in heart,
for they shall see God.

MATTHEW 5:8

What is meant by *blessed?* Some say it is little more than a synonym for "happy," but it is much deeper than that. . . . The Greek term that is translated "blessed" was used to describe two different conditions. First, it was used to describe the . . . wealthy who, by virtue of their riches, lived above the normal cares and worries of lesser folk. Second, the term was also used to describe the condition of the Greek gods who, because they had whatever they desired, existed in an unbelievable state of well-being, satisfaction, and contentment. . . .

By repeating the same word to His band of simple-hearted, loyal followers, [Jesus] reassured them that enviable qualities such as delight, contentment, fulfillment, and . . . joy were theirs to claim. . . . He promised that by tossing aside all the extra baggage that accompanies religious hypocrisy and a performance-oriented lifestyle, we will travel the road that leads to inner peace. In doing so, we become "blessed."

Simple Faith

Do the Good You Can

Do not withhold good from those to whom it is due,
when it is in your power to do it.

PROVERBS 3:27

Matthew Henry wrote: "Wherever the Providence of God casts us, we should desire and endeavor to be useful; and, when we cannot do the good we would, we must be ready to do the good we can. And he that is faithful in a little shall be entrusted with more."

That thought moves me. If you can't do the good you *would*, do the good you *can*. You may have had big-time plans in your life—major league dreams that haven't panned out. You were going to write a best-selling book, but the opportunities just haven't come along. Are you willing to write for your church newsletter? . . .

Maybe you wanted to teach in seminary or Bible school, but the pressures of life forced you in a different direction. Are you willing to teach a Sunday school class? . . . Maybe you'd hoped to be a missionary . . . but for one reason or another, that door has never opened. . . . Are you open to working with Hispanic or Vietnamese people in your own city?

Moses: A Man of Selfless Dedication

God Is in Control

> *Do not be wise in your own eyes;*
> *fear the LORD and turn away from evil.*
>
> PROVERBS 3:7

🌾 What often looks as if it is here to stay . . . can be frighteningly temporary. When God says, "That's it; that's curtains," it's only a matter of time. It is the perspective in all of this that holds us together. Our God is in complete control. He lets nothing out of His grip. . . .

Yet our Lord is not some tyrannical god who stomps across heaven like the giant in *Jack in the Beanstalk,* swinging a club and waiting to give us a smashing blow to the head. No. Rather it is as if He says to us, "You're Mine, and I want you to walk in step with Me. I've arranged a plan so that walking with Me will result in a righteous lifestyle. If you make a decision not to walk with Me, I've also arranged consequences that will happen and you must live with them."

Yes, life is short. Yes, our sins are obvious. . . . But instead of thinking of these days as just about as futile as emptying wastebaskets, see the significance of them in light of God's plan. . . . He has a way of balancing out the good with the bad.

Living Above the Level of Mediocrity

WISDOM FOR THE WAY   225

Our Job Is to Obey

Let all who take refuge in You be glad,
let them ever sing for joy.

PSALM 5:11

As you walk the path of trust you will experience situations that simply defy explanation. When you look back, after the fact, you could never have figured out a better plan. At the time it seemed strange, mysterious . . . even illogical. Let me assure you, that's God working. Things will happen that seem to be totally contradictory, but these are God's arrangements. It was a wonderful day when I finally realized I don't have to explain or defend the will of God. My job is simply to obey it.

It is a waste of time trying to unscrew the inscrutable workings of God. You'll never be able to do it. That's simply the way God works. He honors faith and obedience. He will honor your faith if you will trust Him in a walk of obedience. And when you trust Him completely, you will enjoy inner quietness and security. You will have a secure confidence that you are walking in His will. You will be surrounded by His peace.

Perfect Trust

A Storehouse of Promises

God made the promise . . .
saying, "I will surely bless you and
I will surely multiply you."

HEBREWS 6:13–14

God's Book is a veritable storehouse of promises—over seven thousand of them. Not empty hopes and dreams, not just nice-sounding, eloquently worded thoughts that make you feel warm all over, but promises. Verbal guarantees in writing, signed by the Creator Himself, in which He declares He will do or will refrain from doing specific things.

In a world of liars, cheats, deceivers, and con artists, isn't it a relief to know there is Someone you can trust? If He said it, you can count on it. Unlike the rhetoric of politicians who promise anybody anything they want to hear to get elected, what God says, God does.

The Finishing Touch

An Unshakable Foundation

Though a host encamp against me,
my heart will not fear; . . .
I shall be confident.

❧ The Hebrew term used by David [in this psalm] and translated "confident" does not mean self-reliant nor brave, humanly speaking. In Hebrew it means "to trust, to be secure, to have assurance." Its Arabic counterpart is picturesque: "to throw oneself down upon one's face, to lie upon the ground." The point here is that the source of David's confidence and stability was not his own strength—but God. His Lord was his only foundation for rock-like stability. What an unshakable foundation!

When pressure mounts, when a groundswell of fear invites panic, to whom do you turn?

Living Beyond the Daily Grind

You Are God's
Personal Concern

When a man's ways are pleasing to the LORD,
He makes even his enemies to be at peace with him.

You know what? God personally cares about the things that worry us. He cares more about them than we care about them: those things that hang in our minds as nagging, aching, worrisome thoughts.

Moses had some worrisome thoughts dragging him down. Do you remember why he left Egypt . . . ? He was running for his life. Pharoah and some of his men were looking for Moses, to kill him. (Exodus 2:15) Then forty years later God told Moses to return to Egypt (Exodus 3 and 4). Naturally Moses was worried about those men back in Egypt who wanted his head. He was reluctant to go back. But once he acquiesced to God's will, he said, "Lord, I'm available. I'm going to trust in You with all my heart. I'm not going to lean on my own understanding." Then while he was still in Midian, God said to him, "Oh by the way Moses, you know all the men who sought your life. They're dead." Isn't that remarkable? What a tremendous relief!

Perfect Trust

All Walls Finally Fall

*He himself is our peace
and has destroyed the barrier,
the dividing wall of hostility.*

EPHESIANS 2:14, NIV

All walls fall . . . eventually. No matter how well-constructed or long-standing it is, the wall will fall. It may be as intimidating as an angry giant or as silent as thin air and just as invisible, like the stubborn will of a person or the bitter spirit of an individual. But all walls finally fall.

Anyone who knows even a little history knows how true that is. To this day, archaeologists' spades continue to unearth the fallen walls of the world's great empire. Egyptians walls. Grecian walls. Roman walls. French walls. German walls. Russian walls. . . .

All walls finally fall. Even our own. Even those built up against us. In the final analysis, Christ conquers! . . . There is no wall so great but that He is not greater still.

Esther: A Woman of Strength and Dignity

An Attitude of Satisfaction

Do not wear yourself out to get rich;
have the wisdom to show restraint.

PROVERBS 23:4, NIV

To the surprise of many people, the Bible says a great deal about money. It talks about earning and spending, saving and giving, investing and even wasting our money. But in none of this does it ever come near to suggesting that money brings ultimate security. . . .

If there were one great message I could deliver to those who struggle with not having an abundance of this world's good, it would be this simple yet profound premise for happiness. For a moment, let's go at it backwards, from right to left.

That which constitutes great wealth is not related to money. It is an attitude of satisfaction ("enough is enough") coupled with inner peace (an absence of churning) plus a day-by-day, moment-by-moment walk with God. Sounds so simple, so right, so good, doesn't it? In our world of more, more, more . . . push, push, push . . . grab, grab, grab, this counsel is long overdue. In a word, the secret is *contentment.*

Strengthening Your Grip

Hope Revived

I hope in You, O LORD;
You will answer, O LORD my God.

PSALM 38:15

Take from us our wealth and we are hindered. Take our health and we are handicapped. Take our purpose and we are slowed, temporarily confused. But take away our hope, and we are plunged into deepest darkness . . . stopped dead in our tracks, paralyzed. Wondering, "Why?" Asking, "How much longer? Will this darkness ever end? Does He know where I am?"

Then the Father says, "That's far enough," and how sweet it is! Like blossoms in the snow, long-awaited color returns to our life. The stream, once frozen, starts to thaw. Hope revives and washes over us.

Inevitably, spring follows winter. Every year. Yes, including this one.

The Finishing Touch

The Urgency of the Hour

I am coming quickly;
hold fast what you have, so that
no one will take your crown.

If you live in the light of Christ's return each day of your life, it does wonders for your perspective. If you realize that you must give account for every idle word and action when you stand before the Lord Jesus, it does amazing things to your conduct. It also makes you recognize how many needless activities we get involved in on this earth. Sort of like rearranging the deck chairs on the *Titanic*. Don't bother! Don't get lost in insignificant details! He's coming soon! Recognize the urgency and the simplicity of the hour!

Hope Again

Pleasure and Pain

> *O my God, in You I trust,*
> *do not let me be ashamed; do not*
> *let my enemies exult over me.*
>
> PSALM 25:2

It's impossible to pass through life without experiencing times when you cannot see your way through a deep valley. Times when the package delivered at the back door comes delivered in the ugly wrapping of death or affliction or illness or even divorce. . . . John Selden, the old British jurist and scholar, put it even more bluntly. "Pleasure is nothing else but the intermission of pain."

You may find yourself enjoying the intermission. Today, you may be smiling. Your heart may be light and merry. Perhaps answers to prayer have come beautifully and deliberately. You are swept away in delight. But it's also quite possible that you are caught in the grip of affliction. You may be going through some of the hardest days of your life. You may be wondering *Why? Why me? Why this trial?*

When you persevere through a trial, God gives you a special measure of insight. You become the recipient of the favor of God as He gives to you something that would not be learned otherwise.

Perfect Trust

Look Heavenward

*The ways of a man are before
the eyes of the LORD, and
He watches all his paths.*

PROVERBS 5:21

God is exacting in His knowledge. . . . Not one detail escapes His attention. . . . He knows everything about us. We are an open book before Him. Furthermore, He is immutably faithful. And yet He deliberately surprises us with difficult assignments, premature or unexpected deaths, lost jobs, and disappointing circumstances along the journey, even while we're in the nucleus of His will. Let's face it, it's a mystery. . . .

Wherever you are in this journey called life, wherever you may be employed, wherever you may be in your domestic situation, wherever you may be in your age, your health, or your lifestyle, God may be preparing you for a great surprise in order to find you faithful. Rather than running from Him, let me suggest the opposite: run *toward* Him. . . . Look heavenward and realize that this arrangement is sovereignly put together for your good and for His glory.

The Mystery of God's Will

Tender and Tolerant

The fountain of wisdom is a bubbling brook.

PROVERBS 18:4

❀ *How far you go in life depends on your being tender with the young, compassionate with the aged, sympathetic with the striving, and tolerant of the weak and the strong. Because someday in life you will have been all of these.*—GEORGE WASHINGTON CARVER.

I have admired those words for years. They reflect a perspective easily forgotten in a dizzy schedule of demands and deadlines. It is easy in such a scene to become shortsighted, to think that now is forever. But those who sustain a close companionship with wisdom tend to be more tender, compassionate, sympathetic, and tolerant than those whose world revolves around themselves.

With wisdom comes depth and stability. When we navigate through life under full sail with wisdom at the helm, we may not miss all of the storms, but we will have the strength to persevere. We can face the unforeseen without the fear of sinking.

Growing Wise in Family Life

A Light for the Path

*Your word is a lamp to my feet
and a light for my path.*

PSALM 119:105, NIV

A healthy fear of God will do much to deter us from sin. When we have a proper fear of the living Lord, we live a cleaner life. Any born-again person who sins willfully has momentarily blocked out his fear of God. You and I can do that. When we actively engage in sin, we consciously put aside what we know to be the truth about God. We suppress the knowledge of Him in our hearts and minds. We lie to ourselves by saying, "We'll get by. God won't mind so much." . . .

I must say that this wholesome fear of the Almighty has turned up missing in our era. And when it is absent, we think we may do as we please. You can live as you please if you know you're not being seen and you won't get caught. But if, down deep inside, you know there is a living and holy God who will not let you get away with sin, you will avoid sin at all costs.

Moses: A Man of Selfless Dedication

Choose Your Attitude

He who trusts in his own heart is a fool,
but he who walks wisely will be delivered.

This may shock you, but I believe the single most significant decision I can make on a day-to-day basis is my choice of attitude. It is more important than my past, my education, my bankroll, my successes or failures, fame or pain, what other people think of me or say about me, my circumstances, or my position. Attitude . . . keeps me going or cripples my progress. It alone fuels my fire or assaults my hope. When my attitudes are right, there's no barrier too high, no valley too deep, no dream too extreme, no challenge too great for me.

Yet, we must admit that we spend more of our time concentrating and fretting over the things that can't be changed in life than we do giving attention to the one thing that can, our choice of attitude.

Strengthening Your Grip

Wisdom

God's wisdom is practical.
It is designed to work for us.

You Lost. Get Over It.

Accept one another,
just as Christ also accepted us
to the glory of God.

ROMANS 15:7

❦ If you don't get your way, get over it, get on with life. If you don't get your way in a vote at a church, get over it. The vote was taken (if the church has integrity, the vote was handled with fairness), now get on with it. Just press on. And don't rehearse the fight or the vote year after year. The work of God slows down when we are not big enough to take it on the chin and say, "We lost!" Having been raised in the South, I didn't know the South lost the Civil War until I was in junior high school . . . and even then it was debatable among my teachers.

Be big enough to say, "We lost." Grace will help.

The Grace Awakening

Shared Joy Is Double Joy

> *Two are better than one because*
> *they have a good return for their labor.*
>
> ECCLESIASTES 4:9

There's an old Swedish motto that hangs in many a kitchen: "Shared joy is a double joy. Shared sorrow is half a sorrow." . . . The secret of survival is not simply enjoying life's joys and enduring its sorrows, it is in sharing both with others.

We gain perspective by having somebody at our side. We gain objectivity. We gain courage in threatening situations. Having others near tempers our dogmatism and softens our intolerance. We gain another opinion. We gain what today, in our technical world, is called "input."

In other words, it is better not to work or live one's life all alone. It's better not to minister all alone. It's better to have someone alongside us in the battle. For that reason, during my days in the Marines, we were taught that if the command "dig in" were issued, we should dig a hole large enough for two.

Living on the Ragged Edge

God Never Leads Us Astray

O LORD, lead me in your righteousness; . . .
make Your way straight before me.

🌿 God's voice isn't all that difficult to hear. In fact, you almost have to be closing your eyes and stopping your ears to miss it. He sometimes shouts through our pain, whispers to us while we're relaxing on vacation, occasionally He sings to us in a song, and warns us through the sixty-six books of His written Word. It's right there, ink on paper. Count on it—that book will never lead you astray.

In addition to His unfailing source of wisdom, He has given you wise counselors, friends, acquaintances, parents, teachers, and mentors who have earned your love and respect through long years. Screen what you believe to be the will of God through their thoughts, their perspectives. Does your conviction about the direction you're headed grow, or are you seeing lots of red flags and caution signs? Before you undertake a major life-direction change, be very careful that it is God's voice, that it is God's call you are hearing.

Moses: A Man of Selfless Dedication

Knowing Your Child

*Educate a child according to
his life requirements; even when he
is old he will not veer from it.*

PROVERBS 22:6, MLB

When it comes to rearing children, developing a strong home where happiness and harmony can flourish, there is a primary starting point: *knowing* your child. This is the most profound insight, the single most helpful secret I can pass on to you on the subject of child-rearing.

Do not think that just because you have conceived, carried, and finally given birth to your little one, you automatically know your child. Nor can you say you know him or her just because you live in the same house. I must say, categorically, *you do not*. Knowing your child takes time, careful observation, diligent study, prayer, concentration, help from above, and, yes, wisdom. Notice I did not include in that list a high IQ or some course in school. The two essential ingredients are desire and time. If you really want to know, and if you're willing to invest the time, God will honor your efforts. He will enable you to know your child.

Growing Wise in Family Life

A Place for Prayer

Therefore, let everyone who is godly pray to You.

PSALM 32:6

Never underestimate the place of prayer. . . . I'm convinced that one of the reasons we are so lax in prayer is that we have never prepared a place to meet with God. When you want to draw near to the heart of God, you have to get away from the din, away from the confusion, away from the noise and distractions. . . . You need a place apart—a place where you can separate yourself from the distractions of daily life and meet, alone, with God. . . .

Then, be specific in your prayer life. If you need a job, pray for a job. If you're an engineer, ask God to open up an engineering position for you, or something related for which you are qualified. . . . If you need fifteen hundred dollars for tuition, ask or that amount. If some fear has you in its grasp, name that fear and ask specifically for relief from it. . . . "We need," as one of my mentors used to say, "to guard against the slimy ooze of indefiniteness." . . .

Make your petitions specific.

Elijah: A Man of Heroism & Humility

Joy Throughout Our Days

If a man should live many years,
let him rejoice in them all.

ECCLESIASTES 11:8

Happiness is for today. Joy is available now. We are not to put it on hold. Happiness isn't something that will secretly open up to us when we turn fifty-five, or when we reach some goal or find the right marriage partner. Happiness is for *now*. It is inseparably linked to the living Lord.

A catechism in the Presbyterian church begins with the question, "What is the chief end of man?" The answer to that question is familiar to many: "The chief end of man is to love God and enjoy Him forever." Not just serve Him, not just obey Him, not just sacrifice to Him, not simply commit ourselves to Him, but enjoy Him—"laugh through life with Him." Smile in His presence. So much more is included in enjoying Him forever than most would ever believe. . . .

Happiness is to pervade all the years of our life. We don't have to wait until we reach some magical age when we are allowed to crack open the door and slip silently into the realm of happiness. It's there for us to enjoy *throughout* our days.

Living on the Ragged Edge

Selfish Desires
or God's Desires?

*The refining pot is for silver
and the furnace for gold,
but the LORD tests hearts.*

PROVERBS 17:3

Ask yourself three questions of discipleship:

As you think through the major decisions you have recently made (during the past six to eight months), have they pleased the Lord or fed your ego?

Have you begun to take your personal goals and desires before the Lord or fed your ego?

Are you really willing to change those goals if, while praying about them, the Lord should lead you to do so?

Discipleship refuses to let us skate through life tossing around a few religious comments while we live as we please. It says, "There can be no more important relationship to you than the one you have with Jesus Christ." And it also says, "When you set forth your goals and desires in life, say no to the things that will only stroke your ego, and yes to the things that will deepen your commitment to Christ."

Strengthening Your Grip

Mercy Beyond Misery

His mercy is upon generation after generation
toward those who fear Him.

LUKE 1:50

I have a dear friend who stayed by his wife's side for almost a year as she was dying with ovarian cancer. He told me of such occasions, when the Lord gave merciful relief from the pain. He said it was almost as if an angel of mercy hovered over their room.

When we're suffering the consequences of unfair treatment, there is mercy with God. When we're enduring the grief of loss, there is mercy. When we struggle with the limitations of a handicap, there is mercy. When we're hurting and in physical pain, there is mercy. All these earthly struggles that occur are no accident. God is in the midst of them, working out His sovereign will. Yes, it's a mystery, which means we need special mercy to endure the anguish and misery of the pain.

The Mystery of God's Will

Developing Inward Beauty

Charm is deceitful and beauty is vain,
but a woman who fears the LORD,
she shall be praised.

PROVERBS 31:30

External beauty is ephemeral. Internal beauty is eternal. The former is attractive to the world; the latter is pleasing to God. Peter describes this inner beauty as a "gentle and quiet spirit" (1 Pet. 3:4). This might be paraphrased "a gentle tranquility." Without question, this is any woman's most powerful quality—true character. And such character comes from within—from the hidden person of the heart—because you know who you are and you know who you adore and serve, the Lord Christ. . . .

Outward adornment doesn't take a great deal of time. I've seen women do it in a few minutes on their way to work in the morning. . . . But it takes a lifetime to prepare and develop the hidden person of the heart.

Hope Again

The Image of God's Son

But we all . . . are being transformed
into the same image from glory to glory,
just as from the Lord, the Spirit.

2 CORINTHIANS 3:18

Maybe you've never before stopped to consider that God is committed to one major objective in the lives of all His people: to conform us to "the image of His Son." We need to blow the dust off that timeless goal now that our cage is overcrowded and our lives are growing increasingly more distant from each other.

Exactly what does our heavenly Father want to develop within us? What is that "image of His Son"? I believe the simple answer is found in Christ's own words. Listen as He declares His primary reason for coming: *For even the Son of Man did not come to be served, but to serve, and to give His life a ransom for many* (Mark 10:45).

No mumbo jumbo. Just a straight-from-the-shoulder admission. He came to serve and to give. It makes sense, then, to say that God desires the same for us.

Dropping Your Guard

A Perfect Plan

He said, "It is finished!"
And He bowed His head
and gave up His spirit.

JOHN 19:30

🌿 Though unbelieving men nailed Jesus to His cross, it occurred "by the predetermined plan and foreknowledge of God." It was exactly at the time and in the place and by the means God had determined. And what looked to the eleven confused disciples as mysterious, as well as unfair and unjust (humanly speaking, it was all of the above and more), God looked at it and said, "That is what I've planned. That's the mission My Son came to accomplish."

That's why Jesus' final words from the cross before He died were "It is finished." God's redemption plan had been completed—Jesus' payment for our sin. And then He slumped in death.

The Mystery of God's Will

Sails Set Toward Joy

A joyful heart makes a cheerful face.

PROVERBS 15:13

🌿 I have discovered that a joyful countenance has nothing to do with one's age or one's occupation (or lack of it) or one's geography or education or marital status or good looks or circumstances. . . . Joy is a choice. It is a matter of attitude that stems from one's confidence in God—that He is at work, that He is in full control, that He is in the midst of whatever has happened, is happening, and will happen. Either we fix our minds on that and determine to laugh again, or we wail and whine our way through life, complaining that we never got a fair shake. We are the ones who consciously determine which way we shall go. . . .

Regardless how severely the winds of adversity may blow, we set our sails toward joy.

Laugh Again

The Will to Do God's Will

Our Father who art in heaven,
Hallowed by Thy name.

MATTHEW 6:9, KJV

By merely reviewing the first few lines of the Lord's Prayer, we gain a renewed respect . . . a healthy and wholesome sense of reverence for our Almighty God and Father. Rather than causing us to run from Him and hide in fear, I find that such an awesome respect makes me want to come close to Him, to wait quietly for Him to work. And so I urge you to slow your pace, to approach His "hallowed name" thoughtfully. Take time! Give Him the respect He deserves. Wait on God. In return, He will give you a clearer vision. Furthermore, He will soften your will and make you want to know and do His will.

Simple Faith

Sensitive Hearts

*The sorrow that is according to
the will of God produces a repentance
without regret, leading to salvation.*

2 CORINTHIANS 7:10

Can you name people today who seem to listen carefully to God—people whose hearts are especially sensitive to the Holy Spirit? I can almost guarantee that those are men and women who know what it is to be broken and bruised. They have the scars to prove it.

Perhaps as you read these words you bear the marks of a carnal week, day after day in which you've gone your own way and grieved the Spirit of God. And now you come to these pages with desperation to change in your heart—to learn from God and renew your fellowship with Him. Do you realize what's happened? Your failure has given you a sensitive, teachable spirit. It has broken the pride barrier in your life. It is what Paul called a "godly sorrow" (2 Cor. 7:10).

Moses: A Man of Selfless Dedication

Give All You Have

*The fear of the LORD is the beginning
of wisdom, and knowledge of
the Holy One is understanding.*

❧ If you're the kind of Christian who really wants the whole purpose of God, then you dare not leave out kingdom commitment. That means your motives must be investigated. For example, every time you make plans to acquire a sizable possession—a car, an expensive boat, a house, and such like—you must deal with it before God and ask: Is this His will? Would this honor Him? Would this glorify Him?

Am I suggesting that you take a vow of poverty? No, not that. My message is not that you go hungry and give up all nice things. I just say you give up *control* of them. Give all you have to the Lord God and trust Him to give back all that you need.

Living Above the Level of Mediocrity

Vision, Vitality, and Victory

Let integrity and uprightness preserve me,
for I wait for You.

PSALM 25:21

🌿 Thoughts are the thermostat that regulates what we accomplish in life. My body responds and reacts to the input from my mind. If I feed my mind upon doubt, disbelief, and discouragement, that is precisely the kind of day my body will experience. If I adjust my thermostat forward to thoughts filled with vision, vitality, and victory, I can count on that kind of day. . . .

Thoughts, positive or negative, grow stronger when fertilized with constant repetition. That may explain why so many who are gloomy and gray stay in that mood . . . and why those who are cheery and enthusiastic continue to be so. . . .

You need only one foreman in your mental factory; Mr. Triumph is His name. He is anxious to assist you. . . . His real name is the Holy Spirit, the Helper.

The Finishing Touch

Hearts to Trust,
Minds to Rest

> *Cast your burden upon the LORD*
> *and He will sustain you; He will never*
> *allow the righteous to be shaken.*

PSALM 55:22

God has entrusted to us a great deal. He knows that we can do all things by His grace, so He's trusting in us to trust in Him. Yet He knows our fears as well, otherwise He wouldn't assure us so often of His purposes and His presence.

We feel hurt and alone—God assures us He cares.
We feel angry and resentful—God provides wisdom and strength.
We feel ashamed—God grants forgiveness and comfort.
We feel anxious—God promises to supply all our needs.

May He give us ears to hear, hearts to trust, and minds to rest in Him. Our God is uniquely and ultimately trustworthy!

Perfect Trust

Slow but Sure

Know that the LORD has
set apart the godly man for Himself;
the LORD hears when I call to Him.

PSALM 4:3

Where are you today on your own journey? Are you discounting the significance of your days? Are you sighing rather than singing? Are you wondering what good can come from all that you have to live with?

We tend to think that if God is really engaged, He will change things within the next hour or so. Certainly by sundown. Absolutely by the end of the week. But God is not a slave to the human clock. Compared to the works of mankind, He is extremely deliberate and painfully slow. As religious poet George Herbert wisely penned, "God's mill grinds slow, but sure." . . .

God's hand is not so short that it cannot save, nor is His ear so heavy that He cannot hear. Whether you see Him or not, He is at work in your life this very moment. God specializes in turning the mundane into the meaningful. . . . One of my longtime friends, Howie Stevenson, often says with a smile, "God moves among the casseroles."

Esther: A Woman of Strength and Dignity

Praise and Adoration

Because Your lovingkindness
is better than life,
my lips will praise You.

PSALM 63:3

Praise is a deeply significant aspect of our personal worship, and we are remiss if we ignore it. . . . We *praise* God by expressing words of honor to Him for His character, His name, His will, His Word, His glory, etc.

Husband, when you were dating your wife-to-be, can you remember doing this? You looked at her hair . . . and you expressed praise over her hair. You praised her for her beauty, her choice of perfume and clothing, and her excellent taste. . . . Praise came naturally because that was a genuine, stimulating part of romance. By the way, I hope you haven't *stopped* praising her! Praise is greatly appreciated by your wife, and likewise by our Lord. . . .

Praise is to flow from within us. Praise is an aspect of prayer—adoration directed to God.

Living Beyond the Daily Grind

We Need Each Other

But now there are many members,
but one body.

1 CORINTHIANS 12:20

Nobody is a whole chain. Each one is a link. But take away one link and the chain is broken.

Nobody is a whole team. Each one is a player. But take away one player and the game is forfeited.

Nobody is a whole orchestra. Each one is a musician. But take away one musician and the symphony is incomplete. . . .

You guessed it. We need each other. You need someone and someone needs you. Isolated islands we're not.

To make this thing called life work, we gotta' lean and support. And relate and respond. And give and take. And confess and forgive. And reach out and embrace.

The Finishing Touch

Solid as Stone

You have been bought with a price:
therefore glorify God in your body.

1 CORINTHIANS 6:20

Committed individuals live with shallow tent pegs. They may own things, but nothing owns them. They have come to terms with merchandise that has a price tag and opted for commitment to values that are priceless.

Denying oneself is not to be equated with losing one's uniqueness or becoming of no value. There have been great people in each generation who modeled self-denial as they made significant contributions to humankind.

For years I taught that we are to "count the cost." It seemed so plausible. But suddenly one day, it dawned on me that Jesus never once told His followers to count the cost. No—He's the One who has already done that. He is the King who has already determined what it will take to encounter and triumph over life's enemies. And what will it take? A few strong, quality-minded champions whose commitment is solid as stone.

Living Above the Level of Mediocrity

Is the Motive Right?

Better is a little with the fear
of the LORD than great treasure
and turmoil with it.

PROVERBS 15:16

Fortune says that to be successful you need to make the big bucks. Why else would the Fortune 500 list make such headlines every year? Anyone who is held up as successful must have more money than the average person.

Understand, there is nothing wrong with money earned honestly. Certainly there is nothing wrong in investing or giving or even spending money if the motive is right, if the heart is pure. But I have yet to discover anyone who has found true happiness simply in the gathering of more money. Although money is not sinful or suspect in itself, it is not what brings lasting contentment, fulfillment, or satisfaction.

Hope Again

A String of Moments

Keep back Your servant from presumptuous sins;
let them not rule over me; then I will be blameless,
and I shall be acquitted of great transgression.

PSALM 19:13

Life on earth is really nothing more than a string of moments, one after another. And I do not want my testimony for Jesus Christ to be shattered by a single moment of indulging my flesh. I don't want *one moment* of rage or pride or arrogance to cast a shadow over a lifetime of walking with my Lord. Frankly, I fear that possibility. And do you know what? I *want* to fear that possibility. When I stop fearing it, I am in grave danger.

The Living Bible renders David's prayer (Ps. 19:13): "Keep me from deliberate wrongs; help me to stop doing them. Only then can I be free of guilt and innocent of some great crime."

What a great prayer! "Lord, you know my capacity to throw everything over in one stupid, fleshly act. Keep me from it! Restrain me. Guard me from trashing it all in one horrible moment of rage or lust. If You guard me and keep me, Lord, I'll never have to look back and mourn over committing such a deed."

Moses: A Man of Selfless Dedication

God Is Bigger
than Our Excuses

Then I heard the voice of the LORD, saying,
"Whom shall I send, and who will go for us?"

❀ We all have excuses to disqualify ourselves
from God's service.

- "I'm not physically well."
- "I've got this temper problem."
- "I can't speak very well in public."
- "I don't have a lot of education."
- "My past is too raunchy!"
- "You see, I'm a divorcee."
- "I was once in a mental hospital."

And on and on and on. . . . But God is bigger
than *any* of those reasons. He specializes in taking
bruised, soiled, broken, guilty, and miserable vessels
and making them whole, forgiven, and useful
again.

You see, God's perspective is much broader
than ours.

Strengthening Your Grip

Stop Running Scared

I trust in the LORD. I will rejoice
and be glad in Your lovingkindness,
because you have seen my affliction;
you have known the troubles of my soul.

PSALM 31:6-7

You may be going through a trial so over-whelming that it's borderline unbearable. You want to see the end of the tunnel. Which is only natural, because once we see that little speck of light, we feel we can make it through to the finish. But God's tunnels are often twisting, too complex and dark to see the light for many days. In such settings He says, "In that dark, twisting, seemingly endless period of time, trust Me. Stop running scared! Stop fearing!"

Perfect Trust

Prayer Is Private Devotion

Pray to your Father who is in secret,
and your Father who sees in secret will repay you.

MATTHEW 6:6

Prayer is never something we do to be seen. It loses its whole purpose if it becomes a platform to impress others. It is a private act of devotion, not a public demonstration of piety. According to Jesus, it belongs in the closet of our lives, an act done in secret. . . .

Christ never saw a prayer as pleading or begging or hammering away at the throne of God. No, the Father knows His children, He knows what we need. Therefore, there is no reason to think that connecting with Him requires special words excessively repeated. . . .

Prayer was never intended to be a verbal marathon for only the initiated . . . no secret-code talk for the clergy or a public display of piety. None of that. Real prayer—the kind of prayer Jesus mentioned and modeled—is realistic, spontaneous, down-to-earth communication with the living Lord that results in a relief of personal anxiety and a calm assurance that our God is in full control of our circumstances.

Strengthening Your Grip

A Position We Can't Fill

Let us not judge one another anymore. . . .

ROMANS 14:13

Each one of us belongs to the same Lord. When we stop dictating, it is easier for others to mature as they follow the Lord's directing.

Freeing others means we never assume a position we're not qualified to fill. This, in one sentence, is enough to stop any person from judging another. We're not qualified. We lack full knowledge. How often we have jumped to wrong conclusions, made judgmental statements, only to find out later how off base we were . . . then wished we could cut out our tongue. What keeps us from being qualified to judge?

We do not know all the facts.

We are unable to read motives.

We find it impossible to be totally objective.

We lack "the big picture."

We live with blind spots.

We are prejudiced and have blurred perspective.

Most of all, we ourselves are imperfect and inconsistent.

The Grace Awakening

A Positive Perspective

I have seen that nothing is better
than that man should be happy in
his activities, for that is his lot.

ECCLESIASTES 3:22

We usually can do very little to change our lot. We can only change our reaction to our lot. We cannot change our past, for example. I don't care how brilliant we are, our past stands in concrete. We cannot erase it. But we can learn today to see our past from God's perspective, and use the disadvantages of yesterday in our life—today and forever.

You and I constantly bump up against people submerged in self-pity. They are hopelessly lost in the swamp of life. And all they can tell you is how wrong this was, or how unfair she was, or how someone's promise was broken, or how that man walked away and left "me and the kids," or that guy broke up a partnership and "took me to the cleaners," and on and on and on.

But Solomon says, in effect, "I suggest to you that there's nothing better than that you look for an advantage and then dwell on it. Make that your life's message. Who knows what impact it will have?"

Living on the Ragged Edge

God's Ways Defy Explanation

*Oh, the depth of the riches of the wisdom
and knowledge of God! How unsearchable his
judgments, and his paths beyond tracing out!*

ROMANS 11:33–34, NIV

The New American Standard declares that last phrase: *"How unfathomable His ways!"* Maybe you've come to discover this in your own experience. You've tried to "trace out His path" and you can't pull it off. You've tried to fathom His "unfathomable" ways and you can't. It just doesn't compute. It blows your microprocessor. You have begun to walk with God like never before in your life, but in that path of obedience, you have come across situations that simply defy explanation—you have encountered situations that seem to be contradictory. That's how God works; accept it! It may not make sense to you for years, if ever. But that's okay. I've come to realize I wouldn't understand His thought processes and planned procedures, even if He took time to explain them to me.

It was a wonderful day for me when I finally realized I don't have to explain the will of God. That's not my task. My job is simply to obey it.

Moses: A Man of Selfless Dedication

Mother's Indelible Impression

Let your father and your mother be glad,
and let her rejoice who gave birth to you.

There is no more influential or powerful role on earth than a mother's. Significant as political, military, education, or religious public figures may be, none can compare to the impact made by mothers. Their words are never fully forgotten, their touch leaves an indelible impression, and the memory of their presence lasts a lifetime. . . .

Abraham Lincoln was right: "No one is poor who had a godly mother." Instead of camping on the negatives and emphasizing how far many mothers have drifted from this magnificent calling to shape the future of our country, I want to throw out a positive challenge. Ladies, this is your hour . . . your distinct opportunity to soar! A harmonious marital partnership and a solid, unselfish commitment to motherhood have never been of greater importance to you or, for that matter, to our nation. Talk about a challenge worth your effort! In spite of what you may have heard, this role is the most dignified, the most influential, and the most rewarding in all the world.

Growing Wise in Family Life

God Supplies Reinforcements

O God the LORD,
the strength of my salvation,
You have covered my head
in the day of battle.

🌿 If you determine to live according to biblical standards, be sure that your enemy is seeking to devour you. You *will* encounter the darts of the devil. Someone put it this way: "Whoever desires to walk with God walks right into the crucible." All who choose godliness live in a crucible. The tests *will* come.

But all is not lost. Far from it! Our great hope and assurance is that the One in us is greater than the one in the world. We do not face such a formidable enemy that we cannot fight him or stand firm and secure in our decision. Our Lord is the God of hope. . . . His supply line never runs short. When His godly followers are in need, He is there to supply the necessary reinforcements. As you do battle, God will provide for all of your needs.

Moses: A Man of Selfless Dedication

Wisdom

*God's wisdom equips us to see
and to handle life as it really is.*

We Need Discipline

*Poverty and shame will come
to him who neglects discipline, but he
who regards reproof will be honored.*

PROVERBS 13:18

Discipline is one of the most hated terms of our times . . . right alongside patience and self-control. But have you noticed how often it comes up in the testimonies of those who win? . . .

Here are some key uses of discipline:

No runner completes the training or a race without it.

No weight-loss program is maintained without it.

No human body is kept fit without it.

No mind is sharpened with it.

No temptation is overcome without it.

If you want to put a stop to mediocrity, to replace excuses with fresh determination and procrastination with tough-minded perseverance, you need discipline.

Day by Day with Charles Swindoll

The Race Is On

*I again saw under the sun
that the race is not to the swift, and
the battle is not to the warriors.*

ECCLESIASTES 9:11

Whenever I scope out the scene here where I live, I observe a large number of people who are pursuing the so-called successful life. They would say the way to make it in this world—the way to succeed—is to increase speed, get stronger, be competitive, think more cleverly, plan longer, and have a visionary strategy—hire people with the skills that are needed and life will be successful. The race is on. Get up earlier. Go to bed later. Make work a top priority. Don't get sentimental about stuff like children, marriage, home, and the family. All that will have to wait. . . . And religion? Leave that for the over-the-hill gang and preachers. . . .

The philosophy of our day will attempt to suck us in and convince us that if we're going to make it, we've got to run faster. . . . We've got to be stronger and more competitive and more clever, even more manipulative. Otherwise, we won't be successful. . . . Don't you believe it!

Living on the Ragged Edge

Salt and Light

God never promised us a rose garden. He came up front with us and admitted that the arena of this world is not a "friend of grace to help us on to God." Nevertheless, strange as it may seem, He went on to tell a handful of Palestinian peasants (and *all* godly servants in *every* generation) that their influence would be nothing short of remarkable. They would be "the salt of the earth" and they would be "the light of the world." And so shall we! So far-reaching would be the influence of servants in society, their presence would be as significant as salt on food and as light on darkness. Neither is loud or externally impressive, but both are essential. Without our influence this old world would soon begin to realize our absence. Even though it may not admit it, society needs both salt and light.

Improving Your Serve

God's Great Faithfulness

Through the LORD's mercies
we are not consumed, because
His compassions fail not.

LAMENTATIONS 3:22

The LORD's mercies never cease.

The LORD's compassions never fail.

The LORD's faithfulness never diminishes.

That defines God's immutability, which is a four-bit word for "He doesn't change." . . . He never cools off in His commitment to us. He never breaks a promise or loses enthusiasm. He stays near us when we are jealous for the truth, and He stays near us when we reject His counsel and deliberately disobey. . . . His faithfulness is unconditional, unending, and unswerving. Nothing we do can diminish it, and nothing we stop doing can increase it. . . . Mysterious though such incredible constancy may seem, it's true,

The Mystery of God's Will

Endurance Finds
Favor with God

*Those . . . who suffer according
to the will of God shall entrust their souls
to a faithful Creator in doing what is right.*

1 PETER 4:19

❦ If you are a hard-working, faithful employee, diligent, honest, productive, prompt, caring, working for a boss who is belligerent, stubborn, short-sighted, and ungrateful, and if you patiently endure that situation—that finds favor with God. . . . When you endure, you put grace on display. And when you put grace on display for the glory of God, you could revolutionize your workplace or any other situation. . . .

The purpose of the believer in society is to bring glory and honor to the name of Christ, not to be treated well or to have life be easy or even to be happy, as wonderful as all those things are. . . .

Why are these things happening to you? So that you might follow in the steps of our Lord Jesus, who suffered for us.

Hope Again

An Endless Litany

*A man will be satisfied with good
by the fruit of his words, and the deeds
of a man's hands will return to him.*

PROVERBS 12:14

While we think we may be immune to the endless litany of television commercials, newspaper ads, our friends' gadgets and gizmos, the constant admonition to spend, spend, spend, we Christians need to be alert to how Satan tempts us with the temporal. I'll mention a few ways to avoid the magnetism of the cash register or the credit card.

Doctrinal danger . . . substituting the temporal for the eternal.

Personal danger . . . trying to impress instead of imparting the Word.

Economical danger . . . spending more than you have.

Psychological danger . . . believing your purchase will make things "all right."

Make Hebrews 12:3 your aim: "Consider Him . . . so that you may not grow weary and lose heart."

Day by Day with Charles Swindoll

Not One Lost Moment

Be careful how you walk,
not as unwise men, but as wise.

God tells us not to be foolish, but wise, making the most of our time, taking every opportunity that comes our way and using it wisely.

Before his twentieth birthday, Jonathan Edwards, the brilliant and godly philosopher-theologian who became God's instrument in the Great Awakening revival of the eighteenth century, resolved "Never to lose one moment of time, but to improve it in the most profitable way I possibly can." That is exactly what he did, using well the intellectual gifts God had given him. He entered Yale at thirteen and at seventeen graduated at the head of his class. At twenty-six he was the minister of one of the largest congregations in Massachusetts. . . .

Following the will of God requires wisdom, clear thinking, and, yes, even good old garden-variety common sense.

The Mystery of God's Will

The Difference
Makes the Difference

*By this all men will know
that you are My disciples, if you
have love for one another.*

JOHN 13:35

✾ If our message is a mirror image of the message
of the world, the world yawns and goes on its way,
saying, "What else is new? I've heard all that since I
was born." But if the Christian lifestyle and motivation and answers are different, the world cannot
help but sit up and take notice, thinking:

How is it that I cannot conquer this habit but
he has?

Why is their love so deep and lasting and ours
so shallow and fickle?

How is it that she can forgive and never hold
a grudge, but I can't get over a wrong? Talk about
kindness and courtesy! These people exude those
things. I wonder why.

I've never seen such integrity. The guy wouldn't
think of taking a dime that isn't his.

Do you get the message? It is the difference
that makes the difference.

Simple Faith

Solitude and Serenity

Make your ear attentive to wisdom,
incline your heart to understanding.

An inner restlessness grows within us when we refuse to get alone [with God] and examine our own hearts, including our motives. As our lives begin to pick up the debris that accompanies a lot of activities and involvements, we can train ourselves to go right on, to stay active, to be busy in the Lord's work. Unless we discipline ourselves to pull back, to get alone for the hard work of self-examination in times of solitude, serenity will remain only a distant dream. How busy we can become . . . and as a result, how empty! We mouth words, but they mean nothing. We find ourselves trafficking in unlived truths. We fake spirituality. . . .

How easy to fall prey to meaningless talk, cliché-ridden responses, and mindless activities! It was never meant to be that way; but, more often than not, that's the way it is. To break the habit, solitude is required. The hard work of self-examination on a recurring basis is absolutely essential.

Intimacy with the Almighty

Happily Ever After?

It is good for me that I was afflicted,
that I may learn Your statutes.

PSALM 119:71

"Happily ever after" belongs at the end of a fairy tale, not in a description of the Christian life. Life in Christ is real. It isn't plastic, it isn't stained-glass, it isn't saccharine, it isn't fantasyland. In all my years of walking with the Lord, I have yet to meet one Christian who has "lived happily ever after." On the other hand, I have met a great many significant saints who have endured affliction, loss, disappointment, setbacks, failures, and incredible pain through the years. And I have seen many of those same men, women, and . . . adolescents cling to their joy, radiate hope, and sustain a winsome spirit . . . even through heartache . . . even through tears . . . even at death's door. . . .

If you're waiting for a seamless, blemish-free week friend, you're going to wait in vain. There is no such thing. And until we learn how to derive lessons from seasons of failure and loss, we'll keep repeating those failures—digging ourselves into an ever deeper hole—rather than moving on as we grow up.

Moses: A Man of Selfless Dedication

When the Going
Gets Rough

*I walk in the way of righteousness,
in the midst of the paths of justice.*

PROVERBS 8:20

Vision is the ability to see God's presence, to perceive God's power, to focus on God's plan in spite of the obstacles.

When you have vision it affects your attitude. Your attitude is optimistic rather than pessimistic. Your attitude stays positive rather than negative. Not foolishly positive, as though in fantasy, for you are reading God into your circumstances. So when a situation comes that cuts your feet out from under you, you don't throw up your arms and panic. You don't give up. Instead, you say, "Lord, this is Your moment. This is where You take charge. You're in this."

This is nothing more than having a strong belief in the power of God; having confidence in others around you who are in similar battles with you; and, yes, having confidence in yourself, by the grace of God. Refusing to give in to temptation, cynicism and doubt. . . . It's hanging tough when the going gets rough.

Living Above the Level of Mediocrity

The Book of Books

He who gets wisdom loves his own soul;
he who keeps understanding will find good.

PROVERBS 19:8

There is something grand about old things that are still in good shape. Old furniture, rich with the patina of age and history, is far more intriguing than the uncomfortable, modern stuff. . . .

The Bible is old also—ancient, in fact. Its timeless stories have for centuries shouted, "You can make it! Don't quit . . . don't give up!" Its truths, secure and solid as stone, say, "I'm still here, waiting to be claimed and applied." Whether it's a prophet's warning, a patriarch's prayer, a poet's psalm, or a preacher's challenging reminder. The Book of books lives on, offering us new vistas. . . .

Though ancient, it has never lost its relevance. Though battered, no one has ever improved on its content. Though old, it never fails to offer something pure, something wise, something new.

The Finishing Touch

Spiritual Fuel

Behold I will pour out my spirit on you;
I will make my words known to you.

What fuel is to a car, the Holy Spirit is to the believer. He energizes us to stay the course. He motivates us in spite of the obstacles. He keeps us going when the road gets rough. It is the Spirit who comforts us in our distress, who calms us in times of calamity, who becomes our companion in loneliness and grief, who spurs our "intuition" into action, who fills our minds with discernment when we are uneasy about a certain decision. In short, He is our spiritual fuel. When we attempt to operate without Him or to use some substitute fuel, all systems grind to a halt.

Flying Closer to the Flame

Do Little Things Well

The commandment is a lamp,
and the teaching is light; and reproofs
for discipline are the way of life.

PROVERBS 6:23

If you want to be a person with a large vision, you must cultivate the habit of doing the little things well. That's when God puts iron in your bones! . . . The test of my calling is not how well I do before the public on Sunday; it's how carefully I cover the bases Monday through Saturday when there's nobody to check up on me, when nobody is looking. . . .

When God develops character, He works on it throughout a lifetime. He's never in a hurry.

It is in the schoolroom of solitude and obscurity that we learn to become men and women of God. It is from the schoolmasters of monotony and reality that we learn to "king it." That's how we become—like David—men and women after God's own heart.

David: Man of Passion and Destiny

Trust Without Reservation

Behold, God is my salvation,
I will trust and not be afraid; for the
LORD GOD *is my strength and my song.*

❧ Christianity is trusting Christ, not self. Most people are trying to reach God, find God, and please God through their own efforts. But perfect trust is resting all of one's weight on something else, not on self. It's like resting on crutches to hold you up when you twist an ankle. You lean on them as your strength. Proverbs 3:5–6 teaches us to "Trust in the LORD with all your heart, and do not lean on your own understanding. In all your ways acknowledge Him, and He will make your paths straight."

In other words, strength comes from proper perspective. Elton Trueblood put it this way, "Faith is not belief without proof, but trust without reservation." Strength comes from choosing to fully trust, pray, and praise. Our circumstances may not change, but in the process we change.

Perfect Trust

Just the Right Message

Let me hear Your lovingkindness
in the morning; for I trust in You.

PSALM 143:8

Listen to me, victims of mistreatment. More importantly, please listen to God's truth. He has a hundred different messages to give you during a hundred different dungeon experiences. He knows just the right message at just the right time, and all it takes to receive it is a sensitive, obedient, trusting heart. Not one preoccupied with revenge or bitterness or hostility, but a heart that says, "Lord, God, help me now. Right at this moment. Deliver me from my own prison. Help me to see beyond the darkness, to see Your hand. As I am being crushed, remold me. Help me to see You in this. . . ."

Pray that prayer. Turn your trial into trust as you look to God to tenderly use that affliction, that dungeon, that abandonment for His purpose. . . .

In the midst of all this, remember, God has not abandoned you. He has not forgotten you. He never left. He understands the heartache.

Joseph: A Man of Integrity and Forgiveness

An Extraordinary Day

I will come like a thief in the night,
and you will not know at what hour
I will come to you.

REVELATION 3:3

🌿 Most of our days begin rather predictably. Day after day, for the most part, we could enter into our diary the same three words: "No big deal." Days don't begin with divine skywriting. . . . Angelic choirs don't waken us with celestial harmony, blending their voices in the "Hallelujah Chorus." . . . However, days that begin uneventfully can also lead into an unbelievable, indescribable series of heart-stopping experiences. Ordinary days, in fact, can become extraordinary. . . .

How about the day Jesus arrived? There wasn't one citizen in Judea who awoke that morning expecting the day to bring such a life-changing event in the village of Bethlehem. . . .

And what about the day . . . of Christ's return? . . . Homemakers will be shopping. Planes will be taking off and landing. . . . Then, suddenly, in the twinkling of an eye, Christ will split the sky, and God's great plan for the future will suddenly take center stage. It could be tomorrow. *It could be today!*

Esther: A Woman of Strength and Dignity

Lord, Keep Me Balanced

Give me neither poverty nor riches;
feed me with the food that is my portion.

PROVERBS 30:8

The longer I live the more I realize the ease with which we can slip into extremes. I see it all around me and sometimes, to my own embarrassment, I find it in myself. A major prayer of mine as I grow older is, "Lord, keep me balanced!"

We need a balance between work and play, between kindness and firmness, between waiting and praying, between saving and spending, between wanting too much and expecting too little, between warm acceptance and keen discernment, between grace and truth.

For many folks, the struggle with imbalance is not an annual conflict—it's a daily grind. . . . The adversary of our souls is the expert of extremes. He never runs out of ways to push us to the limit . . . to get us to go so far out on one end we . . . cast perspective to the winds.

The longer I live, the more I must fight the tendency to go to extremes . . . and the more I value balance.

Living Beyond the Daily Grind

No One Is Insignificant

*The path of the righteous is like
the light of dawn, that shines brighter
and brighter until the full day.*

PROVERBS 4:18

Have you ever noticed how uniquely adapted
each animal is to its environment and its way of
life? On land, a duck waddles along ungainly on its
webbed feet. In the water, it glides along smooth as
glass. The rabbit runs with ease and great bursts of
speed, but I've never seen one swimming laps. . . .

God has placed you in His family and given
you a certain mixture that makes you unique. No
mixture is insignificant!

That mix pleases Him completely. Nobody
else is exactly like you. That should bring you pleasure, too.

When you operate in your realm of capabilities,
you will excel and the whole Body will benefit . . .
and you will experience incredible satisfaction.

The Finishing Touch

Accountable to Each Other

He who listens to reproof
acquires understanding.

PROVERBS 15:32

People who are accountable usually have four qualities:

Vulnerability—capable of being wounded, shown to be wrong, even admitting it before being confronted.

Teachability—a willingness to learn, being quick to hear and respond to reproof, being open to counsel.

Availability—accessible, touchable, able to be interrupted.

Honesty—committed to the truth regardless how much it hurts, a willingness to admit the truth no matter how difficult or humiliating the admission may be. Hating all that is phony or false.

That's a tough list! . . . Today we need others to hold us accountable. Sometimes an objective opinion will reveal a blind spot. Sometimes we may simply need a sounding board to help keep us on target. Just remember—not one of us is an island. We need one another.

Living Above the Level of Mediocrity

Praising Personal Worth

The mouth of the righteous
is a fountain of life; . . . on the lips
of the discerning, wisdom is found.

PROVERBS 10:11, 13

When we say thank you to someone who completes a task, we are expressing our appreciation. But when we acknowledge and express our gratitude for what others are—in character, in motive, in heart—we are affirming them personally. A mark of maturity is the ability to affirm, not just appreciate.

How easy to see people (especially family members and fellow [employees]) as doers of tasks, but a task-oriented mentality is incomplete. As important as appreciation for a job well done may be, it too is incomplete. People aren't human tools appointed to accomplish a set of tasks, but human beings with souls, with feelings. How essential it is to recognize and affirm the unseen, hidden qualities that make an individual a person of worth and dignity.

Laugh Again

Finding Fulfillment

In the way of righteousness is life,
and in its pathway there is no death.

PROVERBS 12:28

The ad campaigns that come out of Madison Avenue promise much more than they can deliver. Their titillating messages fall into four categories: fortune and fame, power and pleasure. . . .

Fortune. Fame. Power. Pleasure. The messages bombard us from every direction. But what's missing in all this? Stop and ask yourself that question. Isn't something very significant absent here?

You bet. A *vertical* dimension. There's not even a hint of God's will or what pleases Him in the hard-core pursuit of success. Note also that nothing in that horizontal list guarantees satisfaction or brings relief deep within the heart. And in the final analysis, what most people really want in life is contentment, fulfillment, and satisfaction.

Hope Again

Focus First on God

*I will give thanks to the L*ORD
*according to his righteousness and will sing
praise to the name of the L*ORD *Most High.*

PSALM 7:17

There is a mystery, an aura about the living God that is designed to force us to trust Him, even when we cannot figure Him out (which is most of the time). . . .

The mystery is purposeful, because His overall plan is profound. . . . His plan is not designed to make us comfortable; it's designed to make us more like Christ, to conform us to His will. . . .

In this life, we have focus choices. We can focus on ourselves, we can focus on our circumstances, we can focus on other people, or we can focus on God. When you think biblically you focus first on God. Regardless of what you want, regardless of the circumstances you're under, regardless of what others say or think, regardless of how you feel, God and God alone is working out His great plan. And in the final tally, it will be fabulous!

The Mystery of God's Will

Get Out of the Rut

A joyful heart is good medicine,
but a broken spirit dries up the bones.

PROVERBS 17:22

Even though our work-week is decreasing and our weekend time is increasing, our country lacks inner peace. External leisure does not guarantee internal rest, does it? Time on our hands, we have. But we don't have meaningful "rest" in the biblical sense of the term. . . .

The answer is [to make] a radical break with the rut of normal living. My good friend Tim Hansel suggests taking different kinds of vacations: midget vacations or mini-vacations (two minutes or more!). Change your routine, my friend. Blow the dust of boredom off your schedule. Shake yourself loose and get a taste of fresh life. Here are several suggestions for adding "zip" to your leisure:

> Begin jogging and/or an exercise program . . .
> Buy a bicycle and start pedaling . . .
> Enroll in a local art class . . .
> Take up a new hobby . . .
> Dig around in the soil, plant a small garden.

Strengthening Your Grip

God Reigns Over All

*Man's steps are ordained by the LORD,
how then can man understand his way?*

Stop and think for a moment about the word *sovereignty*. There's a small word nestled in the heart of it, the word *reign*: sov-*reign*-ty. . . .

Sovereignty means our all-wise, all-knowing God reigns in realms beyond our comprehension to bring about a plan beyond our ability to alter, hinder, or stop.

Let me go further. His plan includes all promotions and demotions. His plan can mean both adversity and prosperity, tragedy and calamity, ecstasy and joy. . . . His plan is at work when we cannot imagine why, because it is so unpleasant, as much as when the reason is clear and pleasant. His sovereignty, though it is inscrutable, has dominion over all handicaps, all heartaches, all helpless moments. . . . Even when we cannot explain the reasons, He understands. And when we cannot see the end, He is there, nodding, "Yes, that is My plan."

The Mystery of God's Will

Trust God for the Next Step

The mind of a man plans his way,
but the LORD directs his steps.

PROVERBS 16:9

❧ Let me pass along an old motto of mind. It's guided me for well over thirty years and remains as appropriate now as the day it first slapped me alongside the head.

I try, I fail.

I trust, He succeeds!

Isn't that true? What simple counsel. Only eight words, yet how profound. Bottom line: If you are moving in the energy of the flesh, you're doomed to fail. The old hymn says it well: "The arm of flesh will fail you, you cannot trust your own." . . . But when you trust the Lord God to give you the next step, when you wait in humility upon Him, *He* will open the doors or close them, and you'll get to rest and relax until He says, "Go."

Moses: A Man of Selfless Dedication

Moral Purity

*The foolishness of man ruins his way,
and his heart rages against the LORD.*

PROVERBS 19:3

❧ It is impossible to come to terms with moral purity without dealing with some practical facts related to the body—our flesh-and-blood appetites that crave satisfaction. Volumes are written about the mind, our emotional makeup, our "inner man," the soul, the spirit, and the spiritual dimension. But by comparison, very little is being said by evangelicals today about the physical body.

We are to present our bodies as living sacrifices to God. (Rom. 12:1)

We are instructed *not* to yield any part of our bodies as instruments of unrighteousness to sin. (Rom. 6:12–13)

Our bodies are actually "members of Christ"; they belong to Him. (1 Cor. 6:15)

You see, these bodies of ours can easily lead us off course. It isn't that the body itself is evil; it's just that it possesses any number of appetites that are ready to respond to the surrounding stimuli . . . all of which are terribly appealing and temporarily satisfying.

Strengthening Your Grip

Perspectives and Preferences

So then we pursue the things which make
for peace and the building up of one another.

ROMANS 14:19

Disagreements are inevitable. . . . There will always be opposing viewpoints and a variety of perspectives on most subjects. Tastes differ as well as preferences. That is why they make vanilla and chocolate and strawberry ice cream, why the build Fords and Chevys, Chryslers and Cadillacs, Hondas and Toyotas. That is why our nation has room for Democrats and Republicans, conservatives and liberals—and moderates. The tension is built into or system. It is what freedom is all about, including religious freedom. I am fairly firm in my theological convictions, but that doesn't mean you (or anyone) must agree with me. All this explains why I place so much importance on leaving "wobble room" in our relationships. One's theological persuasion may not bend, but one's involvements with others must.

The Grace Awakening

Genuine Enjoyment

For who can eat and who can
have enjoyment without Him?

ECCLESIASTES 2:25

When I was growing up, my family lived next door to a family that had many of the world's goods we didn't have, but they didn't have the joys Christ can bring—which we had in abundance. I remember one Christmas when we were singing together as a family. . . .

Suddenly, my mom said, "We're making so much noise; we better close the windows or we'll disturb all the neighbors." So we closed the windows.

Within minutes our phone rang. It was a girl who lived next door. She asked, "Why'd you close the windows?"

"Well, we didn't want to disturb you," was Mom's answer. The girl blurted out, "Disturb us? That's the most laughter we've heard the entire Christmas season! . . . That's beautiful music!" . . .

If you really want to have fun—I mean the kind of fun that is really enjoyment (without a hangover)—then you need . . . a relationship with the living God.

Living on the Ragged Edge

We're All Clay Pots

But we have this treasure in earthen vessels,
so that the surpassing greatness of the power
will be of God and not from ourselves.

2 CORINTHIANS 4:7

Do you know what an earthen vessel is? It's nothing more than a clay pot. . . . That's a reference to our bodies and our abilities in the strength of our flesh. That is all you and I have to offer God . . . a pot. A perishable container.

You may be like brittle, delicate china. You break and chip easily, and you could show the glue marks because of those broken times. Then again, you may be a rugged, scarred hunk of heavy pottery—not very attractive, but boy, are you useful. Or you may be composed of clay that hasn't yet been fired in the kiln; you are still being molded and shaped for use. . . .

To tell you the truth, it isn't the condition of the pot that's most important. What's important is the treasure inside—the light and glory of Christ's salvation. What's a few dings, or even a crack or two? If others can see the glory inside through the cracks, so much the better.

Moses: A Man of Selfless Dedication

Wisdom

*Since wisdom is God's specialty,
it's imperative that we seek it prior
to every major decision.*

Sincere Faith at Home

I am mindful of the sincere faith within you,
which first dwelt in your grandmother Lois,
and your mother Eunice.

2 TIMOTHY 1:5

Paul knew Timothy's heritage. He knew that the things that characterized the grandmother and the mother characterized Timothy. That's the way sincere faith works. . . .

Listen to this, moms! Please read my words carefully. A church, a Christian school, a circle of Christian friends can deposit facts into heads. But they cannot translate truth into authentic living. Those avenues can't make it "real." Truth doesn't weave itself into real fleshed-out life until it flows through you. Kids gather the facts. They learn them from the books. They see it in print on a page. But then they look to you to see it modeled into a sincere kind of faith.

Believe me, we can give our children the words to say, we can convey Christian concepts until we turn a deep shade of blue, but they won't fit reality until our young see the reality of such truths in the home.

Growing Wise in Family Life

In the Shadow of the Savior

Trust in the LORD and do good.

PSALM 37:3

If you wish to be a man or woman of God who desires to live a godly life that will leave its mark upon this world, you must stand in the shadow of your Savior. Trust Him to work through the trials you encounter, through the extreme circumstances you cannot handle on your own. He is still the God of impossible situations. He does what no earthly individual can do.

You must approach the impossible with calmness and contentment, with gentleness and self-control, with faith and humility.

Examine your own life for these character traits and take them one by one before God. You might say . . . , "Lord, today I want to do what You say regarding contentment; I want to have a calm and gentle spirit. I don't simply want to call myself a Christian. . . . Help me this day to face everything and deal with everyone with a gentle and quiet spirit. Help me to be content, even though I don't get things my way. . . ."

That is how we personify a life of faith.

Elijah: A Man of Heroism & Humility

God Does Mysterious Things

[When] I saw every work of God,
I concluded that man cannot discover the work
which has been done under the sun.

ECCLESIASTES 8:17

There are numerous riddles in life that remain wrapped in mystery and shrouded inside an enigma. The sea, for example, is an unexplainable phenomenon. . . . There are diseases that still remain a mystery . . . yet we seem to have little trouble going on through life with dozens of riddles still unanswered, hundreds of mysteries still unsolved. . . .

But when God leaves us with a mystery that isn't solved in a week or two, most of us go through desperate struggles believing that He is good or fair. I mean, after all, if we're going to trust a good God, He should do only good things, right? No fair doing mysterious stuff! . . .

Yet God's Word, like God's will, is full of mysteries. Why should we be surprised, then, when God steps in and does mysterious things? Why should that make us wonder if He is good—or wonder if we want to keep believing? Since when must everything be easily or logically explained?

Living on the Ragged Edge

Don't Expect Approval

> *"Behold, I, even I am bringing the flood of*
> *water upon the earth. . . . But I will establish My*
> *covenant with you; and you shall enter the ark."*
>
> GENESIS 6:17–18

God informed Noah of His plan: He was going to destroy the world with a flood. So for one hundred and twenty years, by faith, Noah followed the Lord's leading. He gathered the materials, he built the ark, probably to the ridicule of everyone around him. After all, this was a world that had never known rain; the earth was watered from beneath. And while Noah was building this ark, he was preaching righteousness to those around him. . . . Surrounded and mocked by his depraved . . . contemporaries, this preacher of righteousness, by faith, stood against the tide of his culture.

Sometimes our faith is such a rebuke to our peers that we suffer persecution because of it. No extra charge for his simple warning: Don't expect overwhelming approval and affirmation just because you've chosen to walk by faith.

The Mystery of God's Will

In the World, Not of It

> *Do not love the world*
> *nor the things in the world.*
>
> 1 JOHN 2:15

If you want to stay clean, even when you're walking alone in the dark, low-ceilinged coal mine of the corrupt and secular culture, you need to remember a few practical things—four come to mind.

1. *Pay close attention to what you look at. . . .* Our eyes seem to be the closest connection to our minds.

2. *Give greater thought to the consequences of sin than to its pleasures. . . .* Nobody ever mentions the ugly underside of pleasurable sins.

3. *Begin each day by renewing your sense of reverence for God.* Start each new day by talking to the Lord, even if that early morning talk has to be brief.

4. *Periodically during each day focus fully on Christ. . . .* Imagine Him as He is thinking about you, praying for you, standing with you, living in you. . . .

Be *in* the world but not *of* it.

Hope Again

God Is Trustworthy

"My thoughts are not your thoughts,
neither are your ways My ways,"
declares the LORD.

ISAIAH 55:8

God is the Potter; we are the clay. He's the Shepherd; we are the sheep. He's the master; we are the servant. No matter how educated we are, no matter how much power and influence we may think we have, no matter how long we have walked with Him, no matter how significant we may imagine ourselves to be in His plan . . . none of that qualifies us to grasp the first particle of why He does what He does when He does it and how He chooses to do it. . . .

The amazing thing is that even in the midst of disappointment, surprise, and mystery you will discover how very reliable and trustworthy God is—and how secure you are in His hands. . . . Puzzling as the process may be to us, He stays with His plan. There is no need for us to know all the reasons, and He certainly doesn't need to explain Himself. Potters work with the clay, they don't fret over it . . . or ask permission to remake the clay into whatever they wish.

The Mystery of God's Will

Choose Joy!

*You will go out with joy
and be led forth with peace.*

ISAIAH 55:12

❀ How do we live with worry and stress and fear? How do we withstand these joy stealers? . . .

Let me be downright practical and tell you what I do. First I remind myself early in the morning and on several occasions during the day, "God, You are at work, and You are in control, And, Lord God, You know this is happening. You were there at the beginning, and You will bring everything that occurs to a conclusion that results in your greater glory in the end." And then? Then (and *only* then!) I relax. From that point on, it really doesn't matter all that much what happens. It's in God's hands. . . .

The pressure on you may be intense. A half-dozen joy stealers may be waiting outside your door, ready to pounce at the first opportunity. However, nothing can rob you of your hold on grace, your claim to peace, or your confidence in God without your permission. Choose joy. Never release your grip!

Laugh Again

Mercy for the Miserable

Blessed are the merciful,
for they shall receive mercy.

MATTHEW 5:10

Mercy is a concern for people in need. It has to do with assisting those less fortunate than ourselves, including those who suffer the consequences of disappointment, disease, and distress. One of my mentors used to say, "Mercy is God's ministry to the miserable." And it does not stop with compassion or sadness over someone in dire straits; it means identifying with those who are hurting and imagining the pain they are having to endure, then doing something about it. . . .

It's not simply some feeling of sympathy or sadness over somebody in trouble, but really getting inside the other person's skin, feeling what *they* feel, understanding *their* misery, and then helping them through it.

Simple Faith

Let God Open the Doors

*In the fear of the LORD
there is strong confidence, and
his children will have refuge.*

PROVERBS 14:26

Do you find yourself trying to hammer a square peg into a round hole? Are you pushing and straining and dumping loads of emotional freight to get something going? You'd better call time out and check with the Coach! When God's in something, it flows.

Let's say you had it in your heart to get into some kind of ministry at your place of employment. You'd like the opportunity to sit down with some co-workers and maybe spend fifteen minutes together around the Scriptures at lunch. Great idea! But don't force it. Lay it before God and let Him open the doors. If He is in it, it's remarkable how approval will be granted, how a growing interest will percolate, and how the timing will fall right into place. It will come together almost in spite of you. . . .

God has no limitations in His ability to pull something off, but He's going to do it in His time and not before.

Moses: A Man of Selfless Dedication

Flexible and Willing

Therefore be imitators of God,
as beloved children, and walk in love,
just as Christ also loved you and
gave Himself up for us.

EPHESIANS 5:1–2

God says we are to be "imitators" of Him, which really means we are to "mimic" Him. Since God is a God of freshness and change, so we should be. . . .

Are you open to change in your life? Are you willing to risk? Are you flexible enough to innovate? Are you willing to tolerate the sheer possibility of making a massive change in your direction for life? "Lord, is it South America? Great! or Indonesia? I'll do it. I'll move or change my profession. Fine! Are You leading me into a new venture? I'll do it. Count me in!"

That's the spirit! It may mean moving across the street. It may mean moving across the States. It may mean moving across the seas. How flexible are you? It may not involve a move at all, only a willingness.

Living Above the Level of Mediocrity

God Loves Us Still

I have loved you with an everlasting love;
therefore I have drawn you with lovingkindness.

JEREMIAH 31:3

From a distance, we dazzle; up close, we're tarnished. Put enough of us together and we may resemble an impressive mountain range. But when you get down into the shadowy crevices . . . the Alps we ain't.

That's why our Lord means so much to us. He is intimately acquainted with all our ways. Darkness and light are alike to Him. No one of us is hidden from His sight. All things are open and laid bare before Him: our darkest secret, our deepest shame, our stormy past, our worst thought, our hidden motive, our vilest imagination . . . even our vain attempts to cover the ugly with snow-white beauty.

He sees it all. He knows our frame. He remembers we are dust.

Best of all, He loves us still.

The Finishing Touch

Biblical Thinking

A man will not be established by wickedness,
but the root of the righteous will not be moved.

PROVERBS 12:3

I want to be quite direct with you. Secular thought has taken a tragic toll on the servant of God's distinctiveness. This has begun to influence the church. Many a believer has surrendered his mind to the world system. The uniquely Christian mind, therefore, is a rare find. Humanism, secularism, intellectualism, and materialism have invaded our thinking to such a marked degree our [testimony] has become diluted—in some cases, nonexistent.

Influenced and impressed by the press, our secularized system of education, shallow social expectations, and the quasi-omnipotent forces of conformity to peer pressure (not to mention the impact of television and movies), Christian servants can easily be caught in the trap. We can literally stop thinking biblically. . . .

Take heed!

Improving Your Serve

God's Pastures Are Green

*We are His people and
the sheep of His pasture.*

PSALM 100:3

❧ I am told that sheep, being stupid animals, frequently are alarmed and actually run over each other, racing away from something that startles them. The shepherd corrects the problem by catching a sheep and gently, yet firmly, forcing it to lie down and feed quietly on the grass beneath its feet. . . .

In our hectic, hurried, harassed age in which headache medications have become the best-selling national product, we must occasionally be made to lie down by our Shepherd-Savior. When He steps into our helter-skelter world, He often forces us to rest. If that has occurred in your life, give thanks— the pastures are green!

Living Beyond the Daily Grind

Stop Running Scared

You, O LORD, are a shield about me,
my glory, and the One who lifts my head.

PSALM 3:3

❀ Did you know that you operate at your poorest when you are scared? A little fear is good for us when danger is present, but a lot of it is demoralizing. It takes away the hope, the dream, the vision, the possibility of overcoming. . . .

Fears lurk in the shadows of every area of life. Perhaps you've suddenly discovered that an unexpected addition to your family is on the way. . . . You may be uncertain where your job is leading. . . . You are uneasy about what's around the corner. Or perhaps you have a doctor's appointment pending and you are afraid of what the exam might reveal. Jesus says, "Stop being afraid. Trust Me!"

Jesus Christ stands at the door. He holds out His hands that are scarred. His feet are pierced, and He bears in His body the marks of death. He says, "I know the pressure you are under. I understand the strain. I know the unfair abuse. But let me offer you some encouragement. Don't be afraid. Look at life through My eyes! Stop letting life intimidate you! Stop running scared. Trust Me!"

Perfect Trust

The Significance of One

I searched for a man among them who should build up the wall and stand in the gap before Me.

EZEKIEL 22:30

🌿 In an overpopulated world, it's easy to underestimate the significance of one. There are so many people who have so many gifts and skills who are already doing so many things that are so important, who needs me? What can I as one individual contribute to the overwhelming needs of our world? Sure is easy to let the vastness of our surroundings do a number on us, isn't it?

But the truth is, you are you—the only you in all the world. . . . You're the only person with your exact heritage, your precise series of events in the pilgrimage and sufferings of life that have brought you to this hour. . . .

When I read God's Word I don't find that many stories about great crusades and . . . mass meetings where God's attention rested on an entire country or a whole community. More often, I find individual men and women who made a difference, who set the pace or cut a wide swath or stood in the gap and changed their times.

Esther: A Woman of Strength and Dignity

Still and Quiet Streams

The LORD is my shepherd . . .
He leads me beside quiet waters.

PSALM 23:1–2

"He leads me beside quiet waters." Look at that phrase. Literally, it refers to waters that have been stilled. Mentally capture the peaceful scene. The sheep are weary and worn. They need a long, refreshing drink from the rapid stream nearby. But sheep are instinctively afraid of running water. . . . Though tired and hot from a blistering day, thirsty sheep will only stand and stare at the fast-flowing stream but never drink.

The shepherd then steps in. With his rod and staff he loosens a few large stones and dams up a place, causing the rushing waters to slow their current. The now quiet waters immediately attract the sheep. In the midst of a rushing stream the shepherd has provided refreshment for the flock with water he has stilled.

Has your Shepherd done this? Has He recently stepped in and made those busy currents of your life a source of refreshment by stilling them, by bringing order out of chaos?

Living Beyond the Daily Grind

Abundant Life

I came that they may have life,
and have it abundantly.

JOHN 10:10

Because it is short, life is packed with challenging possibilities. Because it is uncertain, it's filled with challenging adjustments. I'm convinced that's much of what Jesus meant when He promised us an abundant life. Abundant with challenges, running over with possibilities, filled with opportunities to adapt, shift, alter, and change. Come to think of it, that's the secret of staying young. It's also the path that leads to optimism and motivation.

With each new dawn, life delivers a package to your front door, rings your doorbell, and runs. Each package is cleverly wrapped in paper and big print. One package reads: "Watch out. Better worry about this!" Another: "Danger. This will bring fear!" And another; "Impossible. You'll never handle this one!"

When you hear that ring tomorrow morning, try something new. Have Jesus Christ answer the door.

The Finishing Touch

Eyes Trained on God

If we confess our sins,
He is faithful and righteous
to forgive us our sins. . . .

1 JOHN 1:9

Perhaps the words "very low" paint a picture of bleakness that describes you at this very moment. You have ignored God's warnings and pushed your strong convictions aside as you associated with the wrong crowd. But now you are at the end of your rope. You're discouraged. You have failed miserably. You're thinking, *What a terrible way to live!*

All of us have spent time in that miserable camp called Reaping What Was Sown. En route, there's enough pleasure to make it seem like fun, but when it's all said and one, it's downright awful. . . .

What we need are suggestions that get us back on track. First, you need to openly acknowledge what caused your condition. Openly admit that you have failed to stand alone as a true child of God. . . .

Second, you will not stand alone when outnumbered or stand tall when tested or stand firm when discouraged if your focus remains on the odds. Your eyes must be trained on the Lord. Everything depends on your focus.

Living Above the Level of Mediocrity

WISDOM FOR THE WAY 321

Suffering Simplifies Life

The nearness of God is my good;
I have made the Lord G<small>OD</small> my refuge.

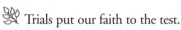 Trials put our faith to the test.

No matter what its source or intensity, there's something about suffering that simplifies life and draws us back to the basics. Invariably, especially during a time of intense trial, . . . I go back to what I really believe. I return to the elementals such as prayer and dependence, like getting quiet and waiting on God. I remind myself, God is sovereign . . . this is no accident. He has a plan and a purpose. Those thoughts give us hope beyond our trials.

Trials put our faith to the test as well as stretch our confidence in Him. They force us back to the bedrock of faith upon which our foundation rests, and this becomes a refining and necessary process.

Hope Again

Simply and Silently

The LORD is good to those who wait for Him, to the person who seeks Him.

LAMENTATIONS 3:25

❧ Spend a full day in quietness. Sundays are great days to do that. Set aside at least part of the afternoon to be completely quiet. Meditation is a lost art in this modern, hurry-up world. I suggest you revive it. Not by endlessly repeating some mantra to get into some other frame of mind. Not that. Simply and silently wait before your faithful God. Read a passage of Scripture, perhaps a psalm, and let it speak. Say nothing. Just sit silently. Let Him talk. Let Him reassure you that you are fully and completely forgiven and that your shame is gone. Feel His arms reach around you. . . . Feel again the freshness and relief of His presence.

The Mystery of God's Will

The Plan in a Child's Heart

*A plan in the heart of a man
is like deep water, but a man of
understanding draws it out.*

PROVERBS 20:5

🌿 To make this verse even more practical, let's think of this "plan" in these terms: "A plan in the heart of a child is like deep water, but a parent of understanding draws it out." . . .

Do you have a child who is mechanically inclined? He needs to know you notice. Make comments about it. Brag on his ability. Do you have a child who is athletic, well-coordinated? He needs to know you believe he is well-coordinated. You say, "That's obvious." But perhaps he hasn't heard it directly from you. He wants to hear you *say it*. You have a child who is intellectually gifted? You sense that she would be good at research, probing deeply into various subjects? *Tell her.* Mention the future possibilities. Help her find the right university. Rather than hammering away on petty stuff that doesn't matter, spend more time discovering how your children's interests can be channeled. Building a strong self-esteem takes a commitment to discover.

Growing Wise in Family Life

Mark Your Meeting Place

My soul waits for the LORD more
than the watchmen for the morning.

PSALM 130:6

To meet regularly with God, you need a place. The house in which I was reared was very small. My mom's place to meet with God was the bathroom. She put her books near the little stove that heated the room. When she met with God she put a little sign on the door that said, "Do not disturb."

Busy mothers can't have their time with the Lord at breakfast or suppertime. That creates havoc. . . . So if you're a mother, you have to be practical about this. Choose a time that works for you, but remember, you need time with God.

If you're a business person, your best place might be at your office. I know a businessman who goes to his office early every weekday morning just so he can spend time with the Lord. . . .

Where is your place? You need such a place where you can sit down and enjoy some uninterrupted fellowship with your Lord. I warn you, if you don't arrange an appropriate place, you probably won't meet regularly with God.

Moses: A Man of Selfless Dedication

Free of Anxiety

Let my prayer come before You;
incline Your ear to my cry!

PSALM 88:2

Our minds can be kept free of anxiety as we dump the load of our cares on the Lord in prayer. By getting rid of the stuff that drags us down, we create space for joy to take its place.

Think of it like this: Circumstances occur that could easily crush us. They may originate on the job or at home or even during the weekend when we are relaxing. Unexpectedly, they come. Immediately we have a choice to make . . . an attitude choice. We can hand the circumstances to God and ask Him to take control or we can roll up our mental sleeves and slug it out. Joy awaits our decision.

Strengthening Your Grip

Take Heart!

> *For God is not unjust so as to*
> *forget your work and the love which*
> *you have shown toward his name.*
>
> HEBREWS 6:10

It is so easy to feel used and unappreciated.

Do I write to you who serve behind the scenes in a ministry or a business? You work faithfully and diligently, yet the glory goes to another. Your efforts make someone else successful. How easy to feel resentful! Assistant directors, associate and assistant pastors, administrative assistants, "internal personnel." All members of the I-work-hard-but-because-I'm-not-up-front-I-never-get-the-credit club, *take heart!* Our God who rewards in secret will never overlook your commitment.

Keep a close eye on your pride. God's true servant is like the Lord Jesus, who came not "to be served, but to serve, and to give His life a ransom for many" (Mark 10:45). . . . When you make the stew and someone else gets the strokes, remember your role: to serve and to give.

Improving Your Serve

The Response of Worship

Though He slay me, I will hope in Him.

JOB 13:15

❧ The more impossible the situation, the greater God accomplishes His work.

This truth is no better illustrated than in the life of Job, a man who went through great times of suffering until God finally brought rest and restoration. When I read the account of Job's plight, I cannot imagine it. He lost everything he owned—his home, all ten of his children, and the loss of his health. It is probably safe to say that not one of us has ever entered into such depths of misery and calamity. Remarkably, his first response to God was the response of worship. "Job arose, tore his robe, shaved his head, and fell on the ground and worshiped" (Job 1:20).

You might expect him to fall to the ground and cry for mercy or to rant and rave that these back-to-back events were simply was not fair. But he didn't. He worshipped. And not because he understood what was happening to him, but in spite of all that was happening to him. Not only did Job worship, he accepted what God had sent into his life. That is wisdom.

Perfect Trust

Discernment and Courage

If you seek [wisdom] as silver
and search for her as for hidden treasures;
then you will discern the fear of the LORD.

PROVERBS 2:4–5

🌿 To have the discernment it takes to refuse the sinful, faith must overshadow feelings. . . .

My feelings say, "Try it!" Faith says, "Stay away from it."

My feelings say, "Give it up. Throw in the towel." Faith says, "Hold on!"

We live in a day of feelings. "Whatever you *feel* like, get at it." The Academy Award-winning song a couple of decades back captured that philosophy with the words, "It can't be wrong, when it feels so right . . ." Oh, yes, it can! Faith says, "Hold it. You have come to a fork in the road. If you take that journey, you will buy into a lifestyle that is wrong. Stop. Back up. Look again."

Maybe you find yourself right there. You have already made some poor choices. If so, it's time to back up. . . . Retrace your steps right back to that place where you made the wrong turn. That takes discernment and courage.

Moses: A Man of Selfless Dedication

Genuine Encouragement

A man has joy in an apt answer,
and how delightful is a timely word!

PROVERBS 15:23

All of us need encouragement—somebody to believe in us. To reassure and reinforce us. To help us pick up the pieces and go on. To provide us with increased determination in spite of the odds. . . .

When we encourage others we spur them on, we stimulate and affirm them. It is helpful to remember the distinction between appreciation and affirmation. We appreciate what a person *does,* but we affirm who a person *is.* Appreciation comes and goes because it is usually related to something someone accomplishes. Affirmation goes deeper. It is directed to the person himself or herself. . . .

I do not care how influential or secure or mature a person may appear to be, genuine encouragement never fails to help. Most of us need massive doses of it.

Strengthening Your Grip

Accountability Is Wise

[There is] a time to embrace,
and a time to shun embracing.

ECCLESIASTES 3:5

There are occasions when we need the embrace of a friend who pulls our head close and whispers in our ear words of understanding, encouraging us not to quit, reminding us that life will go on . . . we will make it. Such embraces put steel into our bones. They help us make it through the night.

And then there are times when that same person may take us by the shoulders, hold us at arm's length, and confront us with the hard truth, "Now listen to this, I can't agree with you. I must be honest with you . . . I think what you are doing is wrong." That is not a time for embracing. But for a life to stay balanced, both affirmation and accountability are needed.

The longer I live, the more I want to listen to wise people. Not so much intelligent people as wise people. A person who is wise not only has intelligence, but understands life and can help put it all together.

Living on the Ragged Edge

A Listening Heart

Hear, O My people, and I will speak.

PSALM 50:7

Mark it down, things do not "just happen." Ours is not a random, whistle-in-the-dark universe. There is a God-arranged plan for this world of ours, which includes a specific plan for you. And through every ordinary day and every extraordinary moment, there is a God who constantly seeks you.

You're walking through [life] and you suddenly encounter one event among the countless myriad of events that happen every day and every night. All of a sudden, life changes. Something's different. And never doubt it! The God who loves us and redeemed us uses those moments to advance His purposes.

He doesn't speak vocally from heaven, shouting down His Word at you. He uses His Book, He uses His people, and He uses events in your life. And through the blending of those unusual events, He says, "Listen to Me. . . . Pay attention, and I will speak to you. Answer My call, and I will use you."

All that is needed is a hushed spirit and a listening heart.

Moses: A Man of Selfless Dedication

Held in Highest Regard

When the LORD your God brings you into
the land . . . then watch yourself, lest you
forget the LORD who brought you . . .
out of the house of slavery.

DEUTERONOMY 6:10, 12

God's got our good at heart. After giving, giving, giving so many things, He warns us about forgetting Him. How easy, when blessed, to adopt a presumptuous, arrogant spirit. Indulgence begins an erosion within that leads to indifference, which ultimately results in independence. "Who needs God any longer?" It is an attitude often found among the self-sufficient. The secret of keeping that from happening? "You shall fear only the Lord you God and you shall worship Him."

When we maintain a sincere fear of God, something wonderful occurs within. Self-made pride and presumption continue to decrease as fear of God increases. I do not mean fright . . . feeling uneasy and afraid in His presence. The right kind of fear is reverence for His holy name, a wholesome respect for His sovereign will, holding Him in highest regard.

Growing Wise in Family Life

God Is There and
He Is Not Silent

*Wise men, and their deeds are in the
hand of God. Man does not know whether it
will be love or hatred; anything awaits him.*

Regardless of rank, status, color, creed, age, heritage, intelligence, or temperament, the "hand of God" is upon us. The late philosopher-theologian Francis Schaeffer was absolutely correct: "God is there and He is not silent." What reassurance this brings! It tells us, among other things, that nothing is out of control. Nor are we useless, despairing robots stumbling awkwardly through time and space, facing a bleak fate at the end. But neither does this mean we are given periodic briefings about His strategy. . . .

Being in the hand of God is not synonymous with or a guarantee for being economically prosperous, physically healthy, protected from pain, . . . and having everyone smile and appreciate us. What helps is the knowledge that behind whatever happens is a God who cares, who hasn't lost a handle on the controls.

Living on the Ragged Edge

Wisdom

*Wisdom preserves our lives from
human pitfalls, and provides our lives
with divine perspective.*

God's Gracious Love

Bless the LORD, O my soul, . . .
Who crowns you with loving-kindness
and compassion.

PSALM 103:1, 4

❧ The sovereign Most High God is ruler over our lives. So it's obvious that if we ever have the feeling of relief, God has given it to us. He's the author of relief. He's the one who grants us the peace, the satisfaction, the ease. In fact, I think relief is a wonderful synonym for mercy. Mercy is God's active compassion, which He demonstrates to the miserable. When we are in a time of deep distress and God activates His compassion to bring about relief, we've experienced mercy. . . .

The connecting link between a holy God and a sinful person is God's love, which activates His grace, which, in turn, sets in motion His mercy. They're like divine dominoes that bump up against one another. He loves us not because of something in ourselves but because of something in Himself. . . . Grace prompts mercy . . . and there it is: *relief!*

The Mystery of God's Will

"Someday" May Never Come

There is an appointed time for everything.
And there is a time for every event under heaven.

ECCLESIASTES 3:1

Remember me? I'm the guy who promotes waiting. Allowing the Lord to open the doors, clear the way, smooth the path, shove you through. You know, all the stuff you expect a preacher to say.

But I do think we can get so good at waiting that we never act. We yawn and passively mutter, "Maybe, someday" as we let opportunities slip away. Like having friends over for ice cream or going on a picnic. Like using the fine china or celebrating a birthday . . . or slipping away for a weekend of relaxation and romance . . . or sailing for a day . . . or spending a week away from the family. "Not this year . . . but maybe, someday . . ."

Don't wait! If you continue such passivity, someday will never come—and you'll regret it for the rest of your days.

Day by Day with Charles Swindoll

The Preparation Process

As high as the heavens are above
the earth, so great is His lovingkindness
toward those who fear Him.

PSALM 103:11

How does the servant of God cope when the bottom drops out? I have found great help from two truths:

Nothing touches me that has not passed through the hands of my heavenly Father. Nothing. Whatever occurs, God has sovereignly surveyed and approved. We may not know why (we may *never* know why), but we do know our pain is no accident to Him who guides our lives.

Everything I endure is designed to prepare me for serving others more effectively. Everything. Since my heavenly Father is committed to shaping me into the image of His Son, He knows the ultimate value of this painful experience. It is a necessary part of the preparation process. It is being used to empty our hands of our own resources, our own sufficiency, and turn us back to Him—the faithful Provider.

Improving Your Serve

An Excellent Wife

An excellent wife, who can find? . . .
Her husband . . . praises her.

PROVERBS 31.10, 28

A wife is not responsible for her husband's life. She is responsible for her life. You cannot make your husband something he is not. Only God can do that.

I think it was the evangelist's wife, Ruth Graham, who once said, "It is my job to love Billy. It is God's job to make him good." I'd call that a wonderful philosophy for any wife to embrace.

Wife, it's your job to love your husband. It's God's job to change his life.

And wives who are truly obedient to Christ will find that He will honor their secure spirit.

Hope Again

God's In Charge

I am the LORD, and there is no other;
the One forming light and creating darkness,
causing well-being and creating calamity.

ISAIAH 45:7

❧ I don't know why a tornado destroys one neighborhood and not another. I just know that even in this calamity God's plan is not frustrated or altered. Either that, or He isn't God. He isn't sitting on the edge of heaven, wondering what will happen next. That's not the God of the Scriptures. So while we cannot fathom the "Why?" of this age-old question, we do know that Scripture states that God is not surprised by calamity. Somehow or other, it's all part of His mysterious will.

Now that's a tough concept to justify. So my advice is quite simple: Quit trying. . . . Remember, nothing is a surprise to God, not even our slightest trials. His plan may seem unfair, humanly illogical, and lacking compassion, but that's because we dwell in the here and now. We lack the vertical view. . . . God's in charge, not us!

The Mystery of God's Will

An Unselfish Attitude

> *Do nothing from selfishness*
> *or empty conceit, but with*
> *humility of mind.*
>
> PHILIPPIANS 2:3

How is it possible to pull off an unselfish attitude when we find ourselves surrounded by quite the opposite? . . . Three practical ideas may help:

1. Never let selfishness or conceit be your motive. That's right, *never*. . . .

2. Always regard others as more important than yourself. Though this is not a natural trait, it can become a habit—and what an important one!

3. Don't limit your attention to your own personal interest—include others.

Some may try to dissuade you from what may appear to be an unbalanced, extremist position. They may tell you that anyone who adopts this sort of attitude is getting dangerously near self-flagellation and a loss of healthy self-esteem. Nonsense! The goal is that we become so interested in others and in helping them reach their highest good that we become self-forgetful in the process.

Laugh Again

Enough Is Enough

The reward of humility and the fear of the LORD are riches, honor and life.

PROVERBS 22:4

❧ I'm not interested in how much your make or what choices you make regarding your lifestyle. Who am I to judge another? My concern really has nothing to do with what you own but rather with why you own it. . . . Can you honestly say that your heart is not fixed on tangible treasures? Is your giving generous? Do you readily help others, even as you enjoy God's gracious provisions? Are you genuinely unselfish, openhanded, greathearted . . . ?

I do not know of a more pronounced idol in this generation than "Sir Greed." I'm convinced it is more powerful and certainly more popular than lust. . . . If you are determined to simplify your life, you will need to ask yourself some hard questions: Why do you want that second job? Why are you working such long hours? Why have you deliberately put your family on hold while you play Russian roulette with greed? When will you be able to say, "Enough"?

Simple Faith

God Bends Over to Listen

I have called upon You,
for You will answer me, O God;
incline Your ear to me, hear my speech.

PSALM 17:6

So many of us feel as though we have to hide our failures, believing no one else could possibly have failed as we have. Some are even afraid to tell God about it, fearing He might be as put off as we imagine others will be.

But He isn't like that at all, is He? When we take a tumble and cry out to Him in our shame and our distress, the psalmist says He "inclines His ear" to us. He bends over to listen. We say, "Oh, Father, I've failed! I've failed terribly. Look at what I've done!" And then He puts His arms around us, just as a loving earthly father would do. He then says, "I accept you just as you are. I acknowledge that what you have done was wrong, as you've confessed it to Me. Now, My son, My daughter, let's move on."

Moses: A Man of Selfless Dedication

Thoughts of Excellence

*We are taking every thought
captive to the obedience of Christ.*

2 CORINTHIANS 10:5

The secret of living a life of excellence is merely a matter of thinking thoughts of excellence. Really, it's a matter of programming our minds with the kind of information that will set us free. Free to be all God meant us to be. . . .

Since the mind holds the secrets of soaring, the enemy of our souls has made the human mind the bull's-eye of his target. His most insidious and strategic moves are made upon the mind. By affecting the way we think, he is able to keep our lives on a mediocre level. . . .

God is interested in our breaking free from such locks.

And what is God's ultimate goal?—To take "every thought captive." When He invades those lofty areas, His plan is to transform the old thoughts that defeat us into new thoughts that encourage us.

Living Above the Level of Mediocrity

Father of Mercies

Blessed be the God and Father
of our Lord Jesus Christ, the Father
of mercies and God of all comfort.

2 CORINTHIANS 1:3

In our world of superficial talk and casual relationships, it's easy to forget that a smile doesn't nec-
essarily mean "I'm happy" and the courteous
answer "I'm fine" may not be at all truthful. . . .

I'm not suggesting that everyone is an emotional time bomb or that masks are worn by all
who seem to be enjoying life. But I've lived long
enough to know that many a heart hides agony
while the face reflects ecstasy.

There is Someone, however, who fully knows
what lurks in our hearts. And knowing, He never
laughs mockingly and fades away. He never shrugs
and walks away. Instead, He understands completely and stays near. . . .

He is "the Father of mercies and the God of all
comfort."

The Finishing Touch

Our Shepherd Leads the Way

I am the good shepherd;
the good shepherd lays down
His life for the sheep.

JOHN 10:11

We, as God's sheep, are sometimes led by Him into the valley of darkness, where there is fear, danger, uncertainty, and the unexpected. He knows that the only way we can reach the higher places of Christian experience and maturity is not on the playground of prosperity but in the schoolroom of suffering. Along those dark, narrow, pinching, uncomfortable valleys of difficulty we learn volumes! We keep our courage simply because our Shepherd is leading the way. Perhaps that is what the writer had in mind when he exhorted us to keep "fixing our eyes on Jesus. . . . for consider Him . . . so that you may not grow weary and lose heart" (Heb. 12:2–3).

Living Beyond the Daily Grind

Open Hands, Open Hearts

But if we hope for what we do not see,
with perseverance we wait eagerly for it.

ROMANS 8:25

That word *persevere* is very important. It's an archaic word and we don't hear much about it in our day of bailing out and giving up. We don't hear much about hanging in there and persevering . . . about staying power! But there is more to it than merely enduring. It's one thing to stand grim-faced, tightfisted, and staring at God with anger, saying, "How DARE YOU! What right do You have?" or "Look at what I've done for you! And look at what I get in return!" That's one kind of perseverance. But there's another kind. The kind that stands with an open hand and open arms, that looks into the face of God and replies, "I submit myself to You. I'm trying hard to hear what You're saying. I wholly and completely admit my dependence. I've run out of answers. I'm waiting."

Perfect Trust

Promote Peace

Like charcoal to hot embers
and wood to fire, so is a contentious
man to kindle strife.

PROVERBS 26:21

A "peacemaker" is the servant who . . . first, is at peace with himself—internally, at ease . . . not agitated, ill-tempered, in turmoil . . . and therefore not abrasive. Second, he/she works hard to settle quarrels, not start them . . . is accepting, tolerant, finds no pleasure in being negative. . . .

Ever been around Christians who are *not* peacemakers? Of course. Was it pleasant? Did you sense a servant's heart? Were you built up and encouraged . . . was the body of Christ strengthened and supported? You know the answers. . . .

Few things are more godlike than *peace*. When we promote it, pursue it, model it, we are linked directly with Him.

Improving Your Serve

God Doesn't Do Standard Things

There is one glory of the sun,
and another glory of the moon,
and another glory of the stars; for
star differs from star in glory.

1 CORINTHIANS 15:41

God is not known for doing standard things. He is engaged in doing very distinct things. When a person does something, it has the man or woman look about it. It drips with humanity. You can follow the logic of it and see the meaning behind it. You can even read what they paid for it and how they pulled it off and the organization that made it so slick. God doesn't build skyscrapers; men build skyscrapers. And they all have the touch of genius, human genius. But you cannot find a man who can make a star. And when God steps in, His working is like the difference between a skyscraper and a star.

Perfect Trust

Focus Fully on God

*Those who wait for the LORD will
gain new strength; they will mount up
with wings like eagles.*

ISAIAH 40:31

We get in a hurry when we don't wait on the Lord. We jump ahead and do rash things. We shoot from the hip. We run off at the mouth, saying things that we later regret. But when we have sufficiently waited on the Lord, He gets full control of our spirit. At such moments, we're like a glove, and His hand is moving us wherever He pleases. . . .

When you wait on the Lord, you don't have to sit in a corner contemplating your navel, or walk around in a daze humming "Sweet Hour of Prayer." You don't have to wear a robe and live in a hut in Tibet for the winter. Sometimes, of course, you need to sit down quietly, by yourself, alone with the Lord for a time of quietness. Solitude and silence are wonderful when nourishing our souls. But mostly you go right on with your business. You press on with your regular activities. You just focus more fully on the Lord in the midst of it. You stay preoccupied with Him. You think His thoughts. . . . You feed your soul His manna.

Esther: A Woman of Strength and Dignity

Endurance Is the Secret

> *Blessed are those who have been*
> *persecuted for the sake of righteousness,*
> *for theirs is the kingdom of Heaven.*
>
> MATTHEW 5:10

Where did Christians get the idea that we'd be appreciated, affirmed, and admired? The Savior Himself taught that blessings are reserved for the persecuted, for those who are reviled, for those against whom folks say all kind of evil . . . falsely . . . (Matt. 5:10–11). It sure is easy to forget those words and get soft, becoming too tender, too sensitive. Fragility is not a virtue extolled in Scripture. Saints with thin skin get distracted and, shortly thereafter, discouraged. There is a long, demanding course to be run, most of which takes place in the trenches and without applause. I suggest we lower our expectations as we intensify our determination and head for the goal.

Endurance is the secret, not popularity.

The Finishing Touch

A Steady Stream of Love

That their hearts may be encouraged,
having been knit together in love.

COLOSSIANS 2:2

What is Christ like? He is characterized by love and forgiveness. An insightful person once said, "We are most like beasts when we kill. We are most like men when we judge. We are most like God when we forgive." . . . Every one of us can blame somebody for something that has happened in our lives. But don't waste your time. What we need most is a steady stream of love flowing among us. Love that quickly forgives and willingly overlooks and refuses to take offense.

Some people are so easy to love that you just naturally fall into their arms. But others are so hard to love, you have to work overtime at it. . . . Some are the opposite of magnets. They repel. Yet even they need our love, perhaps more than the others. How very important that we "stretch fervently" to love each other!

Hope Again

Holiness Is
Part of the Process

Consecrate yourselves . . .
and be holy; for I am holy.

LEVITICUS 11:44

Some people give the impression that we'll never be able to work hard enough to be holy enough. We'll never give up enough things to be holy. At the opposite extreme are those folks who see holiness as entirely passive. God distributes it. He dumps it on you. You enjoy it, take advantage of it, but you're just a passive part of the process.

Let me correct both of these extremes. First of all, we must be holy. Holiness always suggests . . . separateness and difference. God, being holy, is different and separate from all other gods. And we, as His children, must be separate and different as well. . . . We must live lives of ethical integrity and moral excellence. If that were impossible for us, God would never require it of us. But He does. . . .

Second, holiness is not passive. It isn't all up to God. We are active participants in the process. Holiness is part of the process of the will of God for us, His children.

The Mystery of God's Will

Love Yourself,
Love Your Wife

*So husbands ought also to love
their own wives as their own bodies.*

EPHESIANS 5:28

Let that verse sink in, men. The love we are to demonstrate on behalf of our wives is in direct proportion to the love we have for ourselves—not a noisy conceit, but a quiet and deep sense of self-worth. Show me a wife who feels loved and appreciated by her husband and I'll guarantee she is married to a man who properly loves himself. But if she's a wife who sighs and says, "Couldn't somebody teach my husband how to love me!" I can assure you she has a man whose self-esteem is lagging.

Until you have a proper sense of self-love, a healthy and wholesome self-esteem, you are not able freely and fully to love someone else. You don't give yourself to others or consider them valuable if you don't first of all consider yourself worthy. . . . Love draws upon the resourcefulness of one's own esteem in order to have sufficient supply to release it to someone else. It takes personal security to do that.

Growing Wise in Family Life

Sweeter than Honey

How sweet are your words to my taste,
sweeter than honey to my mouth.

PSALM 119:103, NIV

Back before the collapse of the atheistic Soviet Union, my friend John Van Diest represented the Evangelical Christian Publishers Association at the Moscow Book Fair. The authorities had granted them reluctant permission to hand out a limited number of Russian language New Testaments, and long lines of people waited in line to receive a copy. When the supplies were exhausted, one desperately disappointed man asked if he might have one of the empty boxes that had once held those Testaments.

"But there's nothing in there!" John protested. "The Bibles are all gone!" With tears glistening in his eyes, the man replied, "Then I at least want the box." The Bible was so precious to this man that he treasured the cardboard box that had held the Scriptures. May our eyes be opened to the astonishing privilege that is ours to hold the complete written Word of God in our very hands.

Moses: A Man of Selfless Dedication

The Godly
Take God Seriously

As the deer pants for streams of water,
so my soul pants for you, O God.

PSALM 42:1, NIV

Whatever we may say godliness is, it is *not* skin deep. It is something below the surface of a life, deep down in the realm of an attitude . . . an attitude toward God Himself.

The longer I think about this, the more I believe that a person who is godly is one whose heart is sensitive toward God, one who takes God seriously. This evidences itself in one very obvious mannerism: the godly individual hungers and thirsts after God. In the words of the psalmist, the godly person has a soul that "pants" for the living God.

The one who sustains this pursuit may be young or old, rich or poor, urban or rural, leader or follower, of any race or color or culture or any temperament, active or quiet, married or single; none of these things really matter. But what does matter is the individual's inner craving to know God, listen to Him, and walk humbly with Him. As I mentioned, the godly take Him seriously.

Strengthening Your Grip

An Endless Cycle

> *All things are wearisome;*
> *man is not able to tell it. The eye is not satisfied*
> *with seeing, nor is the ear filled with hearing.*

❧ You work so that you can make money, so that you can spend it, so that you can work and make more money, so that you can spend it, so that you can get more, which will mean you spend more, and you'll work harder to make more. So goes this endless cycle. . . .

That explains why people will line up by the millions to view a fantasy on film and sit in silent amazement at someone's imaginary world of imaginary characters who do imaginary things—because life under the sun is so dreadfully, unchangingly boring.

To put it bluntly, life on planet Earth *without* God is the pits. That's the way God designed it. He made it like that. He placed within us that God-shaped vacuum that only He can fill. Until He is there, nothing satisfies. There is no hell on earth like horizontal living without God.

Living on the Ragged Edge

WISDOM FOR THE WAY   357

You're in Good Hands

What does it mean to say that God is faithful? It means He is steadfast in His allegiance to His people. He will not leave us in the lurch. It also means He is firm in his adherence to His promises. He keeps His word. Faithfulness suggests the idea of loyalty: dependability; constancy; being resolute, steady, and consistent. God isn't fickle, no hot-and-cold temperamental moods with Him!

God is also faithful to remember His servants.

He remembers our work—each individual act.

He takes note of the love within us that prompted the deed.

No one on earth can do those special things. We forget, but God remembers. We see the action, God sees the motive This qualifies Him as the best record keeper and judge. He alone is perfectly and consistently just. You're in good hands with the Almighty!

Improving Your Serve

God Renovates Our Souls

Behold, You desire truth in the
innermost being, and in the hidden part
You will make me know wisdom.

PSALM 51:6

God must break through several hard, exterior barriers in our lives before He can renovate our souls. His persistent goal is to break through to the inner person.

What are those resistant layers in our hearts, and how does He break through to that *hidden part?* First, He finds pride. And He uses the sandpaper of obscurity to remove it ever so gradually.

Then He finds us gripped by fear—dread of our past, anxiety over our present, and terror over what may lie ahead—and He uses the passing of time to remove that fear. We learn that things aren't out of hand at all; they're in His hand.

He next encounters the barrier of resentment—the tyranny of bitterness. He breaks down that layer with solitude. In the silence of His presence, we gain a fresh perspective, gradually release our cherished *rights,* and let go of the expectations that held us hostage.

Moses: A Man of Selfless Dedication

Honest-to-Goodness Men

*He who pursues righteousness and
loyalty finds life, righteousness and honor.*

PROVERBS 21:21

I'm concerned about a vanishing masculinity that was once in abundance. I mean honest-to-goodness men who are distinctly that—discerning, decisive, strong-hearted men who know where they are going and are confident enough in themselves (and their God) to get there. They aren't afraid to take the lead, to stand tall and firm in their principles even when the going gets rough.

Such qualities not only inspire the respect of women, they engender healthy admiration among younger men and boys who hunger for heroes. We need . . . more clear-thinking, hard-working, straight-talking men who, while tender, thoughtful, and loving, don't feel the need to ask permission for taking charge. I'm convinced that most single ladies would love to have men like that to spend time with . . . and most wives long to have men like that to share life with. Children especially like having dads like that.

Growing Wise in Family Life

Hearts that Are His

My son, if your heart is wise,
my own heart also will be glad and
my inmost being will rejoice.

PROVERBS 23:15–16

When God's call comes, will He find us ready and willing to stand for Him. Will He find in us hearts that are completely His? Will He be able to say, "Ah, yes, that one's heart is completely Mine. Yes, there's sufficient commitment there for Me to use that life. . . ."

If your Christianity hasn't put that kind of steel in your spine, that quality of marrow in your bones, there's something terribly wrong, either with the message you're hearing or with your heart. God is looking for men and women whose hearts are completely His, men and women who won't blend into the scenery. . . .

What spot has God given you? Whatever it is, God says, "You're standing before *Me*, and I want to use you. I want to use you as My unique spokesperson in your day and age, at this moment and time."

Elijah: A Man of Heroism & Humility

Integrity and Honesty

He stores up sound wisdom for the upright;
He is a shield to those who walk in integrity,
guarding the paths of justice, and He
preserves the way of His godly ones.

PROVERBS 2:7–8

❧ If we walk in integrity, we will not stumble. What a great thought! If we decide that we will live honestly—which means, for example, conducting an honest business—we will not stumble into dishonesty. We will model honesty. God promises He will honor that. He will protect us. That means that ultimately we win over the ungodly. We gain because we're living in the realm of honesty and they're not. He stores up sound wisdom for us. With it, He gives us a shield of protection as we walk in integrity. . . .

God is ready to do His part whenever we're ready to do ours.

Living on the Ragged Edge

Walking by Faith

We would not trust in ourselves, but in God . . . who will deliver us, He on whom we have set our hope.

2 CORINTHIANS 1:9–10

The old motto of soldiers during the Revolutionary War applies to many areas of life: "Trust in God, but keep your powder dry!" In other words, place your life in the Savior's hands, but stay at the ready. Do all that you can to prepare yourself for battle, understanding that the ultimate outcome rests with the Lord God.

To walk by faith does not mean stop *thinking*. To trust God does not imply becoming slovenly or lazy or apathetic. . . . You and I need to trust God for our finances, but that is no license to spend foolishly. You and I ought to trust God for safety in the car, but we're not wise to pass on a blind curve. . . .

Acting foolishly or thoughtlessly, expecting God to bail you out if things go amiss, isn't faith at all. It is presumption. Wisdom says, do all you can within your strength, then trust Him to do what you cannot do.

Moses: A Man of Selfless Dedication

Set Yourself Apart

But like the Holy One who called you,
be holy yourselves also in all your behavior.

1 PETER 1:15

What does it mean to be *holy?* . . . Stripped down to its basics, the term *holy* means "set apart" in some special and exclusive way. . . . In holy matrimony, for example, a man and a woman are set apart, leaving all others as they bond exclusively to each other. . . .

In Holy Communion . . . the bread and wine are set apart from common use and set aside to God alone. The same meaning lies behind the word *sanctify* in 1 Peter 3:15: "But sanctify Christ as Lord in your hearts." . . . We are to "set Him apart" as Lord in our hearts.

What a successful way to deal with the cosmos! To begin the morning by saying, "Lord, I set apart my mind for You today. . . . I set apart every limb of my body and each area of my life unto You as Lord over my life." When we start our day like that, chances are good that temptation's wink will not be nearly as alluring.

Hope Again

Free to Fly

Blessed be the God and Father of our Lord Jesus Christ, who according to his great mercy, has caused us to be born again to a living hope.

1 PETER 1:3

🌿 Grace frees us to fly. So, fly! Dare I give a few illustrations? Aw, why not? You've had your eyes on that sailboat or catamaran or sports car for some time. Why not? You've thought a lot about a cruise or a trip to Europe but never permitted yourself to do more than think. Why not?

Your hairdo has looked the same for three decades. You've wondered about trying something really chic. Why not?

You long to get your degree, but everybody tells you to give up that dream. Should you press on? Why not? . . .

You'd love to throw a big, crazy party with a few happy-go-lucky folks who know how to have fun. Why in the world not?

Grace frees us to fly. So, fly!

Day by Day with Charles Swindoll

Wisdom

We all want to hit the mark,
to live the rest of our lives on target.
But we know that we cannot do it
apart from the wisdom of God.

Shaped by God

But we all . . . beholding as in a mirror
the glory of the Lord, are being transformed
into the same image from glory to glory.

2 Corinthians 3:18

A sculptor was asked how he could carve a lion's head out of a large block of marble. "I just chip away everything that doesn't look like a lion's head," was his reply. God works away in our being and chips away everything that doesn't look like Christ—the impatience, the short temper, the pride, the emotional drives that lead us away from our Father. He's shaping us into His image. That's His predetermined plan. And He's committed to it. Nothing we can do will dissuade Him from that plan. He stays at it. He is relentless. And He never runs out of creative ideas.

That's why he sends one person to the mission field in China and another to the bank building in downtown Seattle. That's part of His sovereign plan to shape individuals into the image of Christ.

The Mystery of God's Will

Infectious Joy

Our mouth was filled with laughter
and our tongue with joyful shouting;
then they said among the nations,
"The LORD has done great things for them."

Perhaps you find yourself among those in the
if-only group. You say you would laugh *if only* you
had more money . . . *if only* you had more talent or
were more beautiful . . . *if only* you could find a
more fulfilling job. I challenge those excuses. Just as
more money never made anyone generous and
more talent never made anyone grateful, more of
anything never made anyone joyful.

Without exception, people who consistently
laugh do so *in spite of*, seldom *because of* anything.
They pursue fun rather than wait for it to knock on
their door in the middle of the day. Such infec-
tiously joyful believers have no trouble convincing
people around them that Christianity is real and
that Christ can transform a life. Joy is the flag that
flies above the castle of their hearts, announcing
that the King is in residence.

Laugh Again

WISDOM FOR THE WAY   369

Depending Wholly on God

Blessed are the poor in spirit,
for theirs is the kingdom of heaven.

MATTHEW 5:3

"Blessed are the poor in spirit." Not poor in substance, but spirit. This first beatitude has nothing to do with being materially destitute or financially bankrupt. Jesus is placing value on a humble spirit, on those who acknowledge a spiritual bankruptcy in and of themselves. Where there is an absence of well-polished pride and personal conceit, there is a wholesome dependence on the living God. Instead of, "No problem, I can handle it . . . ," there is a quick confession, acknowledging one's own inadequacies. . . .

And the promised blessing for such a humble, dependent . . . attitude? "Theirs is the kingdom of heaven," Jesus said. By living lives of such *Simple Faith* beneath our Father's sovereign, gracious care, we truly enter into what kingdom living in all about.

Simple Faith

Getting Acquainted
with Christ

> *[My determined purpose is]*
> *that I may know Him—that I may*
> *progressively become more deeply and*
> *intimately acquainted with Him.*
>
> PHILIPPIANS 3:10, AMP

Like the great apostle Paul, let's make this our "determined purpose." Let's deliberately embrace this aim: to "become more intimately acquainted with Christ." Not intimately acquainted with theology, as important as theology may be. Not intimately acquainted with the church, as valuable as the church may be. Not with sharing Christ with others, as stimulating and significant as evangelism may be. No, none of the above!

With Christ. With Him and Him alone! From this time forward, our goal in life is to become intimately acquainted with Him. I believe this is precisely what Jesus had in mind when He commanded, "Seek first the kingdom of God and His righteousness . . ." (Matt. 6:33, NKJV). . . .

There is nothing—absolutely nothing—of greater importance than knowing Christ intensely and intimately.

Intimacy with the Almighty

Skimming the Treetops

He Himself knows our frame;
He is mindful that we are but dust.

God is mindful that He created us as finite beings out of a few pounds of garden soil. He understands that. . . . My question is, why don't we understand it? Why do we expect perfection of ourselves and of our associates? . . .

You and I become terribly impatient with our own shortcomings and limitations and with each other. We despair because we think we ought to be in spiritual orbit by this time, when we're barely skimming the treetops. . . . We think we ought instantly, constantly, and effectively to conquer vast territories for the kingdom, like some spiritual Alexander the Great. And when it doesn't happen— when victory seems elusive—we grow discouraged.

Whenever I start feeling like that, I need to revisit the life of Moses. . . . Here was a man who didn't become effective for God until he was *eighty*. Long after most of us would be riding a rocking chair or pushing up daisies, Moses began his spiritual career. And guess what? God used him mightily.

Moses: A Man of Selfless Dedication

God's Applause

I have no greater joy than this,
to hear of my children walking in the truth.

3 JOHN 1:4

Great word, *enthusiasm.* Its Greek origin is *entheos,* "God in." It is the ability to see God in a situation that makes it exciting. Do you know that God is watching your life? Do you realize that? Something happens to us when we become convinced that God our heavenly Father is aware of and involved in our activities and is, in fact, applauding our lives.

Think of all you have accomplished to this point. Try to imagine the horizons and challenges of your future. As you mentally travel from the vanishing point of yesterday to the vanishing point of tomorrow you will find that God has been and always will be present. There is not a place in the entire scope of your existence where God is not there.

Living Above the Level of Mediocrity

Prefer Giving

It is more blessed to give than to receive.

Yourself, yourself, yourself, We're up to here with self! Do something either *for* yourself or *with* yourself or *to* yourself. How very different from Jesus' model and message! No "philosophy" to turn our eyes inward, He offers rather a fresh and much-needed invitation to our "me-first" generation. There is a better way. Jesus says, "Be a servant, give to others!" Now that's a philosophy that anybody can understand. And without question, it is attainable.

Stop permitting two strong tendencies—selfishness and conceit—to control you! Let nothing either of them suggests win a hearing. Replace them with "humility of mind." How? By regarding others as more important than yourself. Look for ways to support, encourage, build up, and stimulate the other person. And that requires an attitude that would rather give than receive.

Improving Your Serve

Emmanuel—God with Us

> *Do not be afraid; for behold, I bring you good*
> *news of great joy which will be for all the people;*
> *for today in the city of David there has been born*
> *for you a Savior, who is Christ the Lord.*
>
> LUKE 2:10–11

Christmas comes each year to draw people in from the cold.

Like tiny frightened sparrows, shivering in the winter cold, many live their lives on the barren branches of heartbreak, disappointment, and loneliness, lost in thoughts of shame, self-pity, guilt, or failure. . . .

Then, as the year draws to a close, Christmas offers its wonderful message. Emmanuel. God with us. He who resided in Heaven, co-equal, and co-eternal with the Father and the Spirit, willingly descended into our world. He breathed our air, felt our pain, knew our sorrows, and died for our sins. He didn't come to frighten us, but to show us the way to warmth and safety.

The Finishing Touch

A Dash of Panic

A gentleman in our church was injured on a ski outing and as a result was confined to crutches for many long weeks. Sometimes you would find him panting at the top of a flight of stairs. If you looked at his hands, you would notice they had gotten red and sore. He truly found that leaning on crutches was *exhausting*.

So is leaning on our own understanding! If you want to spend an exhausting day, try to work out your circumstances leaning on your *human viewpoint*. Chase down all the possibilities you can think of. When you hit a dead-end street, back out, then turn down into another one. Drive fast, then slam on your brakes. Throw in a dash of panic, a pinch of fear, add a tablespoon of manipulation, three cups of scheming, and a handful of pills! When you are through, consider where you have been. That is an excellent recipe for "instant depression." Furthermore, you will be mentally exhausted. Peace will flee from you.

Living Beyond the Daily Grind

A Gallery of Memories

*O my God, my soul
is in despair within me;
therefore I remember You.*

PSALM 42:6

Our past is like an art gallery. Walking down those corridors of our memory is like walking through an art gallery. On the walls are all of yesterday's pictures: our home, our childhood, our parents, our rearing, the heartaches, the difficulties, the joys and triumphs as well as the abuses and the inequities of our life. Since Jesus Christ our Lord is the same yesterday and today and forever, then we can take the Christ of today and walk with Him into our yesterday and ask Him to remove the pictures that bring bad or defeating memories. In other words, the Christian can let Jesus invade yesterday and deal with those years of affliction— those years which the locusts have eaten (Joel 2:25–26)—and remove those scenes from the corridors of our lives. I have them. You have them. We need to let Him leave the murals that bring pleasure and victory and take down from the walls those things that bring despair and defeat.

David: A Man of Passion and Destiny

Ask God to Take Charge

We also exult in our tribulations, knowing
that tribulation brings about perseverance.

ROMANS 5:3

One of the Greek terms for "tribulation" in the New Testament refers to "pressure . . . like being crushed under a big boulder." This is a description of pain, of enduring strain. It's an illustration of the crush of our times. There's a certain kind of pressure that comes with unemployment. There's another kind of pressure that comes with the threat of losing your home. There's a pressure that comes from calamity or a wayward child or a runaway mate. . . .

Does God care about the number of hairs in your scalp? Does He care if a sparrow falls? Yes, His Word assures us He does. Then be assured of this: He's a specialist in the things that worry you down inside. The things you dread tomorrow or this coming week. The things that make you wonder, "How can I get this together?" God's reassurance to you is, "Look, that's what I specialize in. I can take that situation you've built into a mountain, and I can bore a tunnel through it in a matter of seconds. Bring all of it to me. Ask Me to take charge."

Perfect Trust

Remember the Right, Forget the Wrong

He who sows righteousness gets a true reward. He who is steadfast in righteousness will attain to life.

PROVERBS 11:18–19

🐦 Whether a personal or public matter, we quickly reveal whether we possess a servant's heart in how we respond to those who have offended us. And it isn't enough simply to say, "Well, okay— you're forgiven, but don't expect me to forget it!" That means we have erected a monument of spite in our mind, and that isn't really forgiveness at all. Servants must be big people. Big enough to *go on,* remembering the right and forgetting the wrong. Like the age-old saying, "Write injuries in dust, benefits in marble. . . ."

True servants, when demonstrating genuine love, don't keep score. Webster defines *forget* as "to lose the remembrance of . . . to treat with inattention or disregard . . . to disregard intentionally: OVER-LOOK: to cease remembering or noticing . . . to fail to become mindful at the proper time." That's the thought.

Improving Your Serve

God's Presence and Power

In God I have put my trust;
I shall not be afraid. What can
mere man do to me?

🌿 We take a look at the money in our pockets and it says, "In God we trust." Trust Him to do what? Keep us free from invasion? Make us prosperous? Sustain our position of world power and leadership? Revolutionary soldiers used to say, "Trust in God but keep your powder dry." Yet as a nation today we are much more self-reliant (keeping our powder dry) than we are God-reliant (trusting in Him).

Here's a direct question: "Can you trust God?" There are two ways to look at that question. Can you *trust* God? That is, is He dependable in times of need? Will He do what He says? Or secondly, we might ask, "Can *you* trust God? Do *you* have such a relationship with Him and such confidence in Him that you believe He is with you always even though you do not see any evidence of His presence and His power?

Perfect Trust

Just Say "No!"

> *Let your heart hold fast my words;*
> *keep my commandments and live.*

Joseph was a good-looking man who, without interest in doing so, caught the eye of [a] woman (Gen. 39:6). . . .

Potiphar's wife was brazenly and shamelessly aggressive [toward him]: "Come to bed with me. Let's have sex" (Gen. 39:7). Most others then and now would have been caught off guard and at least momentarily felt flattered. . . . Not Joseph. Not even for a moment. Without hesitation and being absolutely secure in himself and his God, he responded with equal boldness. . . .

He refused! . . . Don't forget those two wonderful words. Here was an Egyptian woman offering her body and a young Jewish servant being tempted by her bold advance. And so? He refused. He said NO! . . .

How could he do that? Two reasons—his loyalty to his master, Potiphar, . . . and his loyalty to God (Gen. 39:9).

Joseph: A Man of Integrity and Forgiveness

Everyone Is Included

*Let the peace of Christ rule in
your hearts, to which indeed you were
called in one body; and be thankful.*

Colossians 3:15

❧ When the world looks for qualities that will get the job done, the externals get the nod. We like people with charisma, people who have pizzazz, who can put up a good front. I've noticed in the past twenty-plus years, we are looking less and less for integrity and honor and true character in a president. We look for people who look good on television, people who can debate an opponent with great ease and little facial sweat, who can compromise enough to please just about everyone. We prefer the externals. Character we'll do without if we have to, but not those externals. But God passes up the externals and looks for the humble of heart!

We live in a world where we take care of our own. We look out for number one. But God's plan encompasses everyone. Every nation. Every race. All cultures. Huge, highly developed countries, but not excluding the small, struggling ones. His message of *shalom* (peace) through faith in Christ is universal. Unlimited. Without prejudice. Vast!

Esther: A Woman of Strength and Dignity

Make a Difference

What use is it, my brethren,
if someone says he has faith
but he has no works?

JAMES 2:14

Does one person make a difference? Let me ask you, did Christ? God so loved the world that He *did something*. He didn't select a committee. He didn't theorize how great it would be for someone to come to our rescue. He didn't simply grieve over our waywardness and wring His hands in sorrow. He did something! And, in turn, the Son of God said to God the Father, "I will go." He *did something* about it. And that's why we can be saved. We don't believe in a theory; we believe in the person of Christ, who died and rose again that we might live and make a difference.

The question is not simply, what do you think of Christ? The question is, what have you done about what you think?

Esther: A Woman of Strength and Dignity

No Shortcuts

> *Blessed is the man who does not walk*
> *in the counsel of the wicked . . . but his*
> *delight is in the law of the LORD.*
>
> PSALM 1:1, 3

Years ago I read of the construction of a city hall and fire station in a small Pennsylvania community. The citizens were so proud of their new red brick structure—a long-awaited dream come true. Not too many weeks after moving in, however, strange things began to happen. Several doors failed to shut completely and a few windows wouldn't slide open very easily. As time passed, ominous cracks began to appear in the walls. Within a few months, the front door couldn't be locked . . . and the roof began to leak. By and by, the little building that was once the source of great pride had to be condemned. An intense investigation revealed that deep mining blasts several miles away caused underground shock waves that subsequently weakened the earth beneath the building foundation, resulting in its virtual self-destruction.

So it is with compromise in a life. Slowly, almost imperceptibly, one rationalization leads to another, which triggers a series of equally damaging alterations in a life that was once stable, strong, and reliable.

Living Beyond the Daily Grind

Expect the Unexpected

Blessed be the LORD GOD,
the God of Israel, who alone
works wonders.

PSALM 72:18

When it came time for God to send His Son to earth, He did not send Him to the palace of some mighty king. He was conceived in the womb of an unwed mother—a virgin!—who lived in the lowly village of Nazareth.

In choosing those who would represent Christ and establish His church, God picked some of the most unusual individuals imaginable: unschooled fishermen, a tax collector (!), a mystic, a doubter, and a former Pharisee who had persecuted Christians. He continued to pick some very unusual persons down through the ages. In fact, He seems to delight in such surprising choices to this very day.

So, let God be God. Expect the unexpected.

The Finishing Touch

The Goal Is Hope

> *Faith is the assurance of things*
> *hoped for, the conviction of things unseen.*
>
> HEBREWS 11:1

Can you remember a recent "gray slush" day? Of course you can. So can I.

The laws of fairness and justice were displaced by a couple of Murphy's Laws. Your dream dissolved into a nightmare. High hopes took a hike. Good intentions got lost in a comedy of errors, only this time nobody was laughing. . . . You felt like telling Bunyan to move over as you slid down into his Slough of Despond near doubting Castle. . . .

Discouragement may be awful, but it is not terminal.

God has an ultimate goal in mind: that we might have hope. And what leads to such a goal? Two things: perseverance and encouragement from the Scriptures. Again, the goal is hope. God has not designed a life of despondency for us. He wants His people to have hope . . . through endurance and through encouragement from the Scriptures.

Living Above the Level of Mediocrity

One Day at a Time

> *When pride comes, then comes
> dishonor, but with the humble is wisdom.*

People who refuse to get bogged down in and anchored to the past are those who pursue the objectives of the future. People who do this are seldom petty. They are too involved in getting a job done to be occupied with yesterday's hurts and concerns. . . .

I know human nature well enough to realize that some people excuse their bitterness over past hurts by thinking, "It's too late to change. I've been injured and the wrong done against me is too great for me ever to forget it."

But when God holds out hope, when God makes promises, when God says, "It can be done, there are *no exceptions*." With each new dawn there is delivered to your door a fresh, new package called "today." God has designed us in such a way that we can handle only one package at a time . . . and all the grace we need will be supplied by Him as we live out that day.

Improving Your Serve

WISDOM FOR THE WAY   387

Marvels and Mysteries
of the Deep

The Spirit searches all things,
even the depths of God.

1 CORINTHIANS 2:10

Deep things are intriguing. Deep jungles. Deep water. Deep caves and canyons. Deep thoughts and conversations.

There is nothing like depth to make us dissatisfied with superficial, shallow things. Once we have delved below the surface and had a taste of the marvels and mysteries of the deep, we realize the value of taking the time and going to the trouble of plumbing those depths.

This is especially true in the spiritual realm. God invites us to go deeper rather than to be content with surface matters.

Intimacy with the Almighty

Relief Instead of Revenge

A man's discretion makes him slow to anger,
and it is his glory to overlook a transgression.

PROVERBS 19:11

Are you aware of the joy-stealing effect an unforgiving spirit is having on your life? If your bitterness is deep enough, you've virtually stopped living. . . .

It's not worth it. You need to come to terms with this lingering, nagging issue now. The peace and contentment and joy that could be yours are draining away, like water down the drain of an unplugged bathtub. It's time for you to call a halt to the dispute: the disharmony must be defused. . . .

Start by telling God how much it hurts and that you need Him to help you to forgive the offense. . . . Get rid of all the poison of built-up anger and pour out all the acid of long-term resentment. Your objective is clear: Fully forgive the offender. Once that is done, you will discover that you no longer rehearse the ugly scenes in your mind. The revengeful desire to get back and get even will wane, and in its now-empty space will come such an outpouring of relief and a new spirit of joy that you won't feel like the same person.

Laugh Again

The Schoolroom of Life

Test yourselves to see if you are
in the faith; examine yourselves!

2 CORINTHIANS 13:5

Life is a schoolroom. In it, we encounter pop quizzes and periodic examinations. You can't have a schoolroom without tests—at least I've never seen one. . . . Throughout the educational process our knowledge is assessed on the basis of examinations. The curriculum of Christ-likeness is much the same. Our Christian maturity is measured by our ability to withstand the tests that come our way without having them shake our foundation or throw us unto an emotional or spiritual tailspin.

The wonderful thing about God's schoolroom, however, is that we get to grade our own papers. You see, He doesn't test us so He can learn how well we're doing. He tests us so *we* can discover how well we're doing.

Hope Again

The Eternal I AM

Let us fix our eyes on Jesus,
the author and perfecter of our faith.

HEBREWS 12:2, NIV

❧ Until your eyes are fixed on the Lord, you will not be able to endure those days that go from bad to worse.

Fix your eyes on the Lord! Do it once. Do it daily. Do it ten thousand times ten thousand times. Do it constantly. When your schedule presses, when your prospects thin, when your hope burns low, when people disappoint you, when events turn against you, when dreams die, when the walls close in, when the prognosis seems grim, when your heart breaks, *look at the Lord, and keep on looking at Him.*

Who is He? He is Yahweh, the eternal I AM, the sovereign Lord of the universe. He cannot do what is unjust; it is against His nature. He has never lost control. He is always faithful. Changeless. All powerful. All knowing. Good. Compassionate. Gracious. Wise. Loving. Sovereign. Reliable.

Moses: A Man of Selfless Dedication

Think Differently

In the way of righteousness is life,
and in its pathway there is no death.

PROVERBS 12:28

Stop being squeezed in! Quit aping the system of thought that surrounds you, its line of reasoning, its method of operation, its style and techniques! How? By a radical transformation within. By a renewed thought pattern that demonstrates authentic godlikeness. Living differently begins with thinking differently. A life that is characterized by serving others begins in a mind that is convinced of such a life. That explains why that great section of Scripture describing Christ's willingness to take upon Himself the form of a servant begins with the words: "Let this mind be in you, which was also in Christ Jesus . . ." (Phil. 2:5, KJV).

Jesus' life of serving was the outworking of His mind—"unsqueezed" by the world system in all its selfishness—and remains, forever, our example to follow.

Improving Your Serve

God's Ultimate Design

But in the day of adversity consider—
God has made the one as well as the other.

ECCLESIASTES 7:13

❧ The Lord God is just as involved and caring during adversity as during prosperity. The Hebrew term translated "consider" suggests the idea "to examine for the purpose of evaluating." In the hard times—when the bottom drops out, enduring days of financial reversal, or severe domestic conflicts—wisdom allows us to examine, to evaluate with incredible objectivity.

God wants us to walk by faith, not by sight. . . . His ultimate design is nothing short of perfect. He's got a plan, but without operating on the basis of His wisdom, we'll panic and run or we'll stubbornly resist His way.

Living on the Ragged Edge

Mimic God

Do not let your heart envy sinners,
but live in the fear of the LORD always.

PROVERBS 23:17

Since most humans suffer from a lack of balance in their lives, our best counsel on this subject comes from God's Word, the Bible. In that Book, there appears a most unusual command: "Be imitators of God, therefore, as dearly loved children . . ." (Eph. 5:1, NIV). Maybe you never realized such a statement was in the Bible. What a strange command: "Be imitators of God"!

In other words, this is neither a passing thought nor a once-in-a-blue-moon experience. The practice of our being people who "mimic God" is to become our daily habit. We are to do what He does. Respond to life as He responds. Emulate similar traits. Model His style.

Strengthening Your Grip

Sharing Freely

> *If we walk in the Light as He Himself is in the Light, we have fellowship with one another, and the blood of Jesus His Son cleanses from all sin.*
>
> 1 JOHN 1:7

Ancient *koinonia* (fellowship) must have been something to behold. As I try to form a mental picture of it, I come up with this description: *Koinonia* is expressions of authentic Christianity freely shared among members of God's family. It is mentioned about twenty times in the New Testament, and without exception it is invariably expressed in one of two directions.

First, it is used in the sense of sharing something *with* someone such as food, money, supplies, encouragement, time, and concern. And second, it is used in the sense of sharing *in* something with someone, like a project, a success, a failure, a need, a hurt.

The significance of all this is that biblical *koinonia* is *never something done alone.* In other words, God's desire for His children is that we be personally and deeply involved in each other's lives. . . . Our superficial "How ya' doin'" and "Have a nice day" won't cut it.

Strengthening Your Grip

A Servant's Heart

Let a man regard us in this manner,
as servants of Christ and stewards of
the mysteries of God.

1 CORINTHIANS 4:1

A spirit of humility is very rare in our day of strong-willed, proud-as-a-peacock attitudes. The clinched fist has replaced the bowed head. The big mouth and the surly stare now dominate the scene once occupied by the quiet godliness of the "poor in spirit." How self-righteous we have become! How confident in and of ourselves! And with that attitude, how desperately unhappy we are! Christ Jesus offers genuine, lasting happiness to those whose hearts willingly declare:

Nothing in my hand I bring,
Simply to Thy cross I cling.
—AUGUSTUS M. TOPLADY

The indispensable condition of receiving a part in the kingdom of heaven is acknowledging our spiritual poverty. The person with a servant's heart—not unlike a child trusting completely in his parent's provision—is promised a place in Christ's kingdom.

Improving Your Serve

Do What Is Right

*Let us draw near with confidence
to the throne of grace, so that we may receive
mercy and find grace to help in time of need.*

HEBREWS 4:16

Every day we live, we have a choice to do what is right or what is wrong. When we send our young children off to school, we tell them, "Now, sweetheart, you need to know that Mom and Dad won't be there to make your decisions. You will find some kids at school who will encourage you to do what is right and you'll find others who will lead you to disobey and do what is wrong. Make the right choice. Select your friends carefully. Be smart." . . .

Before Christ, we had no choice. Sin was our one and only route. All of life was marked by unrighteousness. But once we came to the Cross and gave the Lord Jesus the right to rule our lives, we were granted a choice we never had before. Grace freed us from the requirement to serve sin, allowing us the opportunity to follow Christ's directives voluntarily. So as long as we do this, *we will not sin!* But as soon as you or I compromise with His mastery over us, the old master stands ready to lure us into sin.

The Grace Awakening

God Promises Wisdom

*If any of you lacks wisdom, let him ask of God
who gives to all generously and without reproach,
and it will be given to him.*

JAMES 1:5

How do we get wisdom? According to James
1:5 we must pray for it. . . . God promises to give
wisdom to us in abundance. It is essential however,
that we ask Him for it.

But praying is just one part of the process in
gaining wisdom. . . . Getting wisdom is the result
of mutual effort. It's a matter of working together
with God in pulling off a wise lifestyle. God doesn't
deliver wisdom at our door like the morning paper.
Wisdom doesn't come in a neat package, like a car-
ton of cool milk that's waiting to be opened. It's the
result of a cooperative effort. . . .

Wisdom doesn't come easily. It may start with
prayer, but there's so much more. To get wisdom,
we must roll up our sleeves. . . . It's like trying to
find hidden treasure; it takes rugged labor. God will
do His part if we'll only do ours. It's a mutual
process.

Living on the Ragged Edge

ACKNOWLEDGMENTS

Grateful acknowledgment is made to the following publishers for permission to reprint this copyrighted material. All copyrights held by the author, Charles R. Swindoll.

Improving Your Serve, (Nashville: Word, 1981).

Strengthening Your Grip, (Nashville: Word, 1982).

Dropping Your Guard, (Nashville: Word, 1982).

Living on the Ragged Edge, (Nashville: Word, 1985).

Living Above the Level of Mediocrity, (Nashville: Word, 1987).

Living Beyond the Daily Grind, (Nashville: Word, 1988).

Living Beyond the Daily Grind, II, (Nashville: Word, 1988).

Growing Wise in Family Life, (Multnomah Press, Portland, Oregon) 1988.

The Grace Awakening, (Nashville: Word, 1990).

Simple Faith, (Nashville: Word, 1991).

Laugh Again, (Nashville: Word, 1992).

The Finishing Touch, (Nashville: Word, 1994).

The Mystery of God's Will, (Nashville: Word, 1993).

Hope Again, (Nashville: Word, 1996).

Intimacy with the Almighty, (Nashville: J. Countryman, 1996).

David: A Man of Passion and Destiny, (Nashville: Word, 1997).

Joseph: A Man of Integrity and Forgiveness, (Nashville: Word, 1998).

Esther: A Woman of Strength and Dignity, (Nashville: Word, 1999).

Moses: A Man of Selfless Dedication, (Nashville: Word, 1999).

Perfect Trust, (Nashville: J. Countryman, 2000).

Elijah: A Man of Heroism and Humility, (Nashville: Word, 2000).

Day by Day with Charles Swindoll, (Nashville: Word, 2000).